D0457449

Life!

BOOKS, AUDIOS, AND VIDEOS
BY LOUISE L. HAY

Books

The Aids Book: Creating a Positive
    Approach
Colors & Numbers
A Garden of Thoughts: My Affirmation
    Journal
Heal Your Body
Heart Thoughts: A Treasury of Inner
    Wisdom
Life! Reflections on Your Journey
Love Your Body
Love Yourself, Heal Your Life Workbook
Loving Thoughts for Health and Healing
Loving Thoughts for Increasing Prosperity
Loving Thoughts for a Perfect Day
Loving Thoughts for Loving Yourself
Meditations to Heal Your Life
101 Power Thoughts
The Power Is Within You
You Can Heal Your Life

Coloring Books/Audiocassettes for Children

Lulu and the Ant: A Message of Love
Lulu and the Dark: Conquering Fears
Lulu and Willy the Duck: Learning
    Mirror Work

Audiocassettes

Aids: A Positive Approach
Cancer: Discovering Your Healing Power
Feeling Fine Affirmations
Gift of the Present with Joshua Leeds
Heal Your Body (Book-on-Tape)
Love Your Body (Book-on-Tape)
Loving Yourself
Meditations for Personal Healing
Morning and Evening Meditations
Overcoming Fears

The Power Is Within You (Book-on-Tape)
Self Healing
Songs of Affirmation with Joshua Leeds
What I Believe/Deep Relaxation
You Can Heal Your Life (Book-on-Tape)
You Can Heal Your Life Study Course

Conversations on Living Lecture Series

Change and Transition
Dissolving Barriers
The Forgotten Child Within
How to Love Yourself
The Power of Your Spoken Word
Receiving Prosperity
Totality of Possibilities
Your Thoughts Create Your Life

Personal Power Through Imagery Series

Anger Releasing
Forgiveness/Loving the Inner Child

Subliminal Mastery Series

Feeling Fine Affirmations
Love Your Body Affirmations
Safe Driving Affirmations
Self-Esteem Affirmations
Self-Healing Affirmations
Stress-Free Affirmations

Videocassettes

Dissolving Barriers
Doors Opening: A Positive Approach to Aids
Receiving Prosperity
You Can Heal Your Life Study Course
Your Thoughts Create Your Life

Available at your local bookstore, or call:
(800) 654-5126

Life!

Reflections on
Your Journey

Louise L. Hay

Hay House, Inc.
Carson, CA

HAY
HOUSE

Copyright © 1995 by Louise L. Hay

Published and distributed in the United States by:

Hay House, Inc., 1154 E. Dominguez St., P.O. Box 6204, Carson, CA 90749-6204
(800) 654-5126

Edited by: Jill Kramer
Designed by: Highpoint Graphics, Claremont, CA

All rights reserved. No part of this book may be reproduced by any mechanical, photographic, or electronic process, or in the form of a phonographic recording, nor may it be stored in a retrieval system, transmitted, or otherwise be copied for public or private use—other than for "fair use" as brief quotations embodied in articles and reviews without prior written permission of the publisher.

The author of this book does not dispense medical advice or prescribe the use of any technique as a form of treatment for physical or medical problems without the advice of a physician, either directly or indirectly. The intent of the author is only to offer information of a general nature to help you in your quest for emotional well-being and good health. In the event you use any of the information in this book for yourself, which is your constitutional right, the author and the publisher assume no responsibility for your actions.

Library of Congress Cataloging-in-Publication Data

Hay, Louise L.
    Life! : reflections on your journey / Louise L. Hay.
        p.   cm.
    Includes bibliographical references.
    ISBN 1-56170-092-4
    1. Conduct of life.   2. Hay, Louise L.   I. Title.
BJ1581.2.H35   1995
158--dc20   95-11990
                                                                              CIP

ISBN 1-56170-092-4

99 98 97 96 95   5 4 3 2 1
First Printing, July 1995

Printed in the United States of America

To my beloved audience that has been with me for so many years, and to those of you who have yet to meet me, I dedicate this book to the enrichment of your lives. May you come with me and learn to make the rest of your days on this beautiful planet Earth the best and most rewarding years of your life.

YOU can help heal our society!

CONTENTS

Chapter

APPENDIX

PREFACE

I decided to write this book as a sequel to both *You Can Heal Your Life* and *The Power Is Within You* because so many people still write me letters and question me in my lectures on the basic questions regarding the meaning of existence, and how we can be the best people we can be in spite of our past experiences, the things that may or may not have been "done" to us, and also in light of our expectations about how the rest of our lives will go. These are people who are working with metaphysical concepts and who are changing their lives by changing their thinking. They are releasing old, negative patterns and beliefs. They are also learning to love themselves more.

Since the title of this book is *Life!*, I have set it up in a loose chronological fashion that mirrors some of the progressions that we go through in life—that is, I start with some of the issues that we face when we are young (childhood issues, relationships, work, and so on) and lead up to the concerns that we have in our elder years.

Now, just in case you're not familiar with my philosophy and the words that I tend to use when I explain those concepts, let me share some of this information with you.

First of all, I often use terms such as *The Universe, Infinite Intelligence, Higher Power, Infinite Mind, Spirit, God, Universal Power, Inner Wisdom,* and so on to refer to that Power that created the Universe and that also resides within you. If you object to the use of any of these terms, in your mind just substitute something else that works for you. After all, it's not the word itself that's important, it's the meaning behind it.

Also, you'll notice that I spell certain words differently than other people do. For example, I always spell the word *disease* as *dis-ease* in order to point out what the word really means and to point out anything that isn't in harmony with you or your environment. Similarly, I never capitalize the word *AIDS,* but spell it with lower case letters: *aids.* I feel it diminishes the power of the word.

As far as my overall philosophy is concerned, I think that it's important for me to go over some of the concepts that I live by even though you may have heard me talk about them before—or, maybe you're new to my work.

Very simply, I believe that what we give out, we get back; we all contribute to, and are responsible for, the events that take place in our lives—both the good and the so-called bad. We create our experiences based on the words we say and the thoughts we think. When we create peace and harmony in our minds and think positive thoughts, we will attract positive experiences and like-minded people to us. Conversely, when we become "stuck" in a blaming, accusing, victim mentality, our lives will be frustrating and unproductive, and we will also attract like-minded people to us. In essence, what I'm saying is that what we believe about ourselves and about life becomes true for us.

Some of the other basic points of my philosophy can be summed up in this way:

- **It's only a thought, and a thought can be changed.**
  I believe that everything in our life began as a thought. No matter what the problem is, our experiences are just outer effects of inner thoughts. Even self-hatred is only hating a thought you have about yourself. For example, if you have a thought that says, "I'm a bad person," then this thought produces a feeling of self-hatred that you buy into. If you didn't have the thought, you wouldn't

have the feeling. Thoughts can be changed. Consciously choose a new thought such as, "I am wonderful." Change the thought, and the feeling changes, too. Every thought we think creates our future.

- **The point of power is always in the present moment.**
  This moment is all we have. What we choose to think and believe and say now is forming the experiences of tomorrow, next week, next month, next year, and so on. When we focus on our thoughts and beliefs right now in the present moment, choosing these thoughts and beliefs with the same care we might select a gift for a special friend, then we are empowered to set a course of our own choosing in our lives. If we are focused in the past, then we don't have a lot of energy to put into the present moment. If we are living in the future, we are living in a fantasy. The only real moment is right now. This is where our change process begins.

- **We must release the past and forgive everyone.**
  We are the ones who suffer when we hold on to past grievances. We give the situations and the people in our past power over us, and these same situations and people keep us mentally enslaved. They continue to control us when we stay stuck in "unforgiveness." This is why forgiveness work is so important. Forgiveness—letting go of the ones who hurt us—is letting go of our identity as the one who was hurt. It allows us to be set free from the needless cycle of pain, anger, and recrimination that keeps us imprisoned in our own suffering. What we forgive is not the act, but the actors—we are forgiving their suffering, confusion, unskillfulness, desperation, and their humanity. As we get the feelings out and let them go, we can then move on.

- **Our minds are always connected to the One Infinite Mind.**
  We are connected to this Infinite Mind, this Universal
  Power that created us, through that spark of light within,
  our Higher Self, or the Power within. The Mind within us
  is the same Mind that directs all of life. Our concern is to
  learn the Laws of Life and to cooperate with them. The
  Universal Power loves all of Its creations, and yet It also
  gives us free will to make our own decisions. It is a Power
  for good, and It directs everything in our lives when we
  allow it. It is not an avenging, punishing power. It is a law
  of cause and effect. It is pure love, freedom, understanding, and compassion. It waits in smiling repose as we
  learn to connect with It. It is important to turn our lives
  over to the Higher Self, because through It, we receive
  our good.

- **Love yourself.**
  Be unconditional and generous in your love for yourself.
  Praise yourself as much as you can. When you realize that
  you are loved, then that love will flood out into all areas
  of your life, returning to you multiplied over and over.
  Therefore, loving yourself will help heal this planet.
  Resentment, fear, criticism, and guilt cause more problems
  than anything else, but we *can* change our thinking patterns, forgive ourselves and others, and learn how to love
  the self, making these destructive feelings things of the past.

- **Each one of us decides to incarnate upon this planet at a
  particular point in time and space to learn lessons that
  will advance us on our spiritual, evolutionary pathway.**
  I believe we are all on an endless journey through eter-
  nity. We choose our sex, our color, our country, and then

we look around for the perfect set of parents who will "mirror" our patterns. All of the events that take place in our lives and all of the individuals we encounter teach us valuable lessons.

Love your life and your self...I do!

— Louise L. Hay
1995, Southern California

INTRODUCTION

Over the last five years or so, I have scaled back on my lecturing and traveling and have now become a farmer of sorts. I spend most of my time in my beautiful garden, which is filled with plants, flowers, fruits, vegetables, and trees of all kinds, and I get enormous pleasure from getting down on my hands and knees, digging around in the soil. I bless the soil with love, and it produces for me abundantly.

I am an organic gardener, so not a single leaf ever leaves my property. Everything goes into the compost pile, and I am gradually building my soil so that it is rich and nourishing. I also eat from my garden as much as possible, enjoying fresh fruits and vegetables all year round.

I'm mentioning my gardening activities here as an introduction to some of the material that I will be presenting in this book. You see, your thoughts are like the seeds you plant in *your* garden. Your beliefs are like the soil in which you plant these seeds. Rich, fertile soil produces strong, healthy plants. Even good seeds struggle to grow in poor soil that is full of weeds and stones.

Gardeners know that when planning a new garden or revamping an old one, the most important thing to do is to prepare the soil. Rocks, debris, weeds, and old, worn-out plants need to be removed first. Then, if you are a serious gardener, you will double-dig down to the depth of two shovels, again removing roots and rocks. Then you add as much organic matter as possible. I am partial to organic compost, horse manure, and fish meal. Three or four inches of these soil amendents and compost are put on top and then dug into the soil and mixed well. Now there is something worth planting in! Anything planted in this soil will shoot up and grow into a strong, healthy plant.

So it is with the soil of our minds, our basic beliefs. If we want new, positive affirmations—that is, the thoughts we think and the words we speak—to become true for us as soon as possible, then we will take the extra effort to prepare our minds to be receptive to these new ideas. We can make lists of all the things we believe (for example, "What I believe about work, prosperity, relationships, health," etc.), and we can examine these beliefs for negativity. You could ask yourself, "Do I want to continue to base my life on these limiting concepts?" Then you can double-dig to eliminate the old ideas that will never support your new life.

When as many of the old, negative beliefs are eliminated as possible, then add a large dose of love and work it into the soil of your mind. Now when you plant new affirmations into your mind, they will sprout amazingly fast. And your life will change for the better so quickly that you will wonder what happened. You see, it is always worth the extra effort to prepare the soil, whether it is in your garden or in your mind.

In this book, each chapter ends with some positive affirmations that pertain to the ideas we have gone over. Select some of those that have meaning for you, and repeat them often. The treatment at the end of each chapter is a flow of positive ideas to help you change your consciousness into a life-affirming belief system. Notice that all treatments and affirmations are done in the first person, in the present tense. We never say, "I will," or "if," or "when," or "as," because these are delaying statements. Whenever we do a treatment or an affirmation, it is always, "I have," "I am," "I always," or "I accept." These are immediate acceptance statements, and the Universe will take care of it NOW!

Please remember that some of the ideas that you will read in the upcoming chapters will be more meaningful to you than others. You might wish to read through the book once and then go back and work with the concepts that make sense to you or that apply to your current life. Repeat the affirmations. Read the treatments. Make these ideas part of you. Later, you can approach the chapters that push your buttons or that you feel couldn't possibly apply to you.

As you get stronger in one area, you'll find that the other areas are easier to work out. And the next thing you know, you'll realize that you're growing from a seedling into a tall, beautiful tree that has its roots planted firmly in the ground. In other words, you'll be flourishing in that complex, magnificent, mysterious, incomparable thing called...

LIFE!

✻ Chapter One ✻

CHILDHOOD ISSUES:
SHAPING US
FOR THE FUTURE

"I look back on the child that I was
with love, knowing that I did the best I could
with the knowledge I had at the time."

My Beginnings

People often look at me at lectures and think, "Oh, she has it all together, she has never had a problem in her life, and she knows all the answers." This is far from the truth. I personally do not know of any good teachers who have not been through many dark nights of the soul. Most of them have come from some incredibly difficult childhoods. It is through the healing of their own pain that they learn how to help others heal their lives.

In my own case, I know that my life was absolutely wonderful, as far as I remember, until I was 18 months old. Then, everything hit the fan for me, especially from my point of view.

My parents suddenly divorced. My mother was an uneducated woman and went to work as a domestic. I was placed in a series of foster homes. My whole world collapsed. There was nothing I could count on and no one to hold me and love me. Finally, my mother was able to get a domestic job where she could have me live with her. But by then the damage was done.

When I was five years old, my mother remarried. Years later she told me that she married so I would have a home. Unfortunately, she married an abusive man, and life became hell for both of us. It was during this same year that I was raped by a neighbor. When this act was discovered, I was told that it was my fault and that I had embarrassed the family. There was a court case, and I still remember the trauma of the medical examination and being forced to testify. The rapist was given a 16-year sentence. I lived in fear of his release because I believed he would come and get me for being such a bad girl as to put him in jail.

I also grew up in the Depression, and we had almost no money at all. There was a neighbor who used to give me ten cents a week, and this money went into the household budget. In those days you could buy a loaf of bread or a box of oatmeal for ten cents. On my birthday and Christmas, she would give me the enormous sum of a dollar, and my mother would go to Woolworth's and buy my underwear and socks for the year. My clothes came from Goodwill. I had to go to school in clothes that did not fit me.

My childhood was one of physical abuse, hard labor, poverty, and ridicule at school. I was made to eat raw garlic every day so I would not get worms. I did not get worms, but I did not get any friends either. I was the girl who smelled and dressed funny.

I now understand that my mother could not protect me then because she could not protect herself. She had also been raised to believe that women accepted whatever men dished out. It took me a long time to realize that this way of thinking did not need to be the truth for me.

As a child, I repeatedly heard that I was stupid, worthless, and ugly—somebody else's no-good brat that had to be fed. How could I possibly feel good about myself when I was constantly being bombarded with negative affirmations? At school I used to stand in the corner and watch the other kids play. I did not feel wanted or needed at home or at school.

When I entered my early teens, my stepfather decided that he would not beat me so much. Instead, he would start going to bed with me. This began a new cycle of horror that lasted until I left home when I was just 15. At that point, I was so starved for love and had such low self-esteem that if some young man put his arms around me, I would go to bed with him. I had no self-worth, so how could I have morals?

When I had just turned sweet 16, I had a baby girl. I only knew her for five days until I handed her over to her new parents. Looking back at that experience now, I realize that the baby needed to find her way to those particular parents, and I was the vehicle to get her there. With my lack of self-esteem and my negative beliefs about myself, I needed the experience of shame. It all fit together.

What We Learn as Children
Affects Who We Will Become

We talk a lot about teenage pregnancy these days and how terrible it is. The point that seems to be missed is that no young girl with self-esteem and self-worth would get pregnant in the first place. If you have been raised to believe that you are a piece of trash, then sexual dis-eases and pregnancy are the logical outcomes.

Our children are our most precious beings, and it is deplorable the way many are treated. At the moment, the largest growing segment of homeless people in this country are mothers with children. It is shameful that mothers sleep on the street and wheel their possessions around in shopping carts. Little children are literally growing up in the streets. Our children are our future leaders. What kind of values will these homeless children have? How can they have respect for others when we care so little for them?

From the moment we are old enough to sit in front of a television set, we are bombarded with sales pitches for products that are often detrimental to our health and well-being. For example, in one half hour of watching children's television, I saw ads for sugar drinks, sugar cereals, cakes and cookies, and lots of toys. Sugar intensifies negative emotions, and it is why little children shriek and scream. These ads may be good for the manufacturers, but they're not good for the children. These ads also contribute to our sense of dissatisfaction and greed. We grow up thinking that greed is normal and natural.

Parents talk about the "terrible two's" and how difficult a period it is. What many people don't realize is that this is the time when the child begins expressing in words the emotions the parents are repressing. Sugar amplifies these repressed feelings. The behavior of small children always mirrors the emotions and feelings of the adults around them. It is the same thing with teenagers and their rebellion. The repressed emotions of the parents have become a burden to the child, and the child outwardly expresses these feelings through rebellion. The parents are looking at their own stuff.

We have allowed our children to sit for hundreds of hours watching violence and crime on TV. Then we wonder why we have so much violence and crime in our schools and among our own young people. We blame the criminal and take no responsibility for our part in contributing to this situation. It's no surprise that we have guns in schools; we see guns on TV all the time. What kids see, they want. Television teaches us to want things.

Much of what we see on television also teaches us to disrespect women and the elderly. Television teaches us very little that is positive. And this is such a shame, because television has the opportunity to contribute to the upliftment of humanity. Television has helped make us into the society we are living in now—one that is often sick and dysfunctional.

Focusing on negativity only causes more negativity. That is why there is so much of it in our world these days. The media—television, radio, newspapers, movies, magazines, and books—all contribute to this focus, especially when they portray violence, crime, and abuse. If the media were to focus on only positive things, after a period of time, crime would dramatically lessen. If we think only positive thoughts, in time our world becomes positive.

We CAN Do Things to Help

There *are* ways in which we can help heal our society. I believe it is essential that we totally stop child abuse at once. Abused children have such low self-esteem that they often grow up to be abusers and criminals. Our prisons are filled with people who were abused as children. And then we self-righteously continue to punish and abuse them as adults.

We cannot build enough jails, or enact enough laws, and take enough action against crime, when the focus is solely on crime and the criminal. I believe our prison system needs a total overhaul. Abuse never rehabilitates anyone. Everyone in prison needs group therapy, both the guards and the inmates. Therapy would be good for the wardens, too. When everyone in the prison system develops self-esteem, society will have gone a long way to becoming healthy.

Yes, I agree that there are some criminals who are beyond rehabilitation and must stay confined. But in most cases, people serve a period of time, and then they are released back into the mainstream. All they have really learned in prison is how to be better criminals. If we could heal their childhood agony and pain, they would no longer need to punish society.

No little baby boy is born an abuser. No little girl is born a victim. This is learned behavior. The worst criminal was once a tiny baby. We need to eliminate the patterns that contribute to such negativity. If we would teach every child that they are worthwhile human beings, deserving of love, if we encouraged their talents and abilities and taught them to think in a way that would create positive experiences, then in one generation we could transform society. These children would be our next parents and our new leaders. In two generations, we would be living in a world where there is respect and caring among all people. Drug and alcohol abuse would be a thing of the past. Doors could remain unlocked. Joy would be a natural part of life for everyone.

These positive changes begin in consciousness. You can contribute to the changes by holding these concepts in your mind. See them as being possible. Meditate every day on transforming our society back to the greatness that is our destiny here in America. You could affirm the following on a regular basis:

> I LIVE IN A PEACEFUL SOCIETY.
> ALL THE CHILDREN ARE SAFE AND JOYFUL.
> EVERYONE IS WELL FED.
> EVERYONE HAS A PLACE TO LIVE.
> THERE IS MEANINGFUL WORK FOR EVERYONE.
> EVERYONE HAS SELF-WORTH AND SELF-ESTEEM.

Understanding Your Inner Child

The first purpose of the soul when it incarnates is to play. The child grieves when it is in an environment where play is not permitted. Many children were brought up needing to ask their parents for everything; they could not make any decisions on their own. Others were raised under the burden of perfection. They were not allowed to make mistakes. In other words, they were not permitted to learn, so now they are fearful of making decisions. All of these experiences contribute to becoming a disturbed adult.

I don't think our current school system helps children to be magnificent individuals. It is too competitive, and yet it also expects every child to conform. I also think the entire testing system in school makes children grow up feeling that they are not good enough. Childhood is not easy. There are too many things that stifle the creative spirit and contribute to feelings of unworthiness.

If you had a very difficult childhood, then today you are probably still rejecting your inner child. Perhaps you are not even aware that inside of you is the unhappy child you once were, one who may still be beating itself up. This child needs healing. This child needs the love you were denied, and you are the only one who can give it.

A good exercise for all of us is to talk to our inner child on a regular basis. I like to take my inner child with me everywhere one day a week. When I awaken, I say, "Hi, Lulubelle. This is our day. Come with me. We are going to have a lot of fun." Then, everything I do that day I do with Lulubelle. I talk to her, out loud or silently, and explain everything we are doing. I tell her how beautiful she is, how smart she is, how much I love her. I tell her all the things she wanted to hear when she was a child. At the end of the day, I feel great, and I know my inner child is happy.

You could find a photo of *yourself* as a child. Put it in a prominent place, perhaps placing some flowers next to it. Whenever you pass the picture, say "I love you; I'm here to take care of you." You can heal your inner child. When that child is happy, then so are you.

You can also write with your inner child. Take out two different-colored pens and a piece of paper. With your dominant hand, the one you always use, write a question. Then with the other pen and your nondominant hand, let your inner child write the answer. It is an amazing way to connect with your inner child. You will get answers that will surprise you.

There is a book by John Pollard III called *Self-Parenting*, which offers a wealth of exercises on how to get in touch with your inner child and how to talk with it. When you are ready to heal, you will find the way.

Every negative message you received as a child can be turned into a positive statement. Let your self-talk be a continual stream of positive affirmations for building self-esteem. You will be planting new seeds that, if well watered, will sprout and grow.

Affirmations for Building Self-Esteem

I AM LOVED AND WANTED.

MY PARENTS ADORE ME.

MY PARENTS ARE PROUD OF ME.

MY PARENTS ENCOURAGE ME.

I LOVE MYSELF.

I HAVE A SMART MIND.

I AM CREATIVE AND TALENTED.

I AM ALWAYS HEALTHY.

I HAVE LOTS OF FRIENDS.

I AM LOVABLE.

PEOPLE LIKE ME.

I KNOW HOW TO MAKE MONEY.

I DESERVE TO SAVE MONEY.

I AM KIND AND CARING.

I AM A TERRIFIC PERSON.

I KNOW HOW TO TAKE CARE OF MYSELF.

I LOVE THE WAY I LOOK.

I AM HAPPY WITH MY BODY.

I AM GOOD ENOUGH.

I DESERVE THE BEST.

I FORGIVE ANYONE WHO EVER HURT ME.

I FORGIVE MYSELF.

I ACCEPT MYSELF AS I AM.

ALL IS WELL IN MY WORLD.

❀ ❀ ❀

I AM PERFECT EXACTLY AS I AM

I am neither too much nor too little. I do not have to prove to anyone or anything who I am. I know I am the perfect expression of the Oneness of Life. In the Infinity of Life, I have been many identities, each one a perfect expression for that particular lifetime. I am content to be who and what I am at this time. I am perfect as I am, right here and right now. I am sufficient. I am one with all of Life. There is no need to struggle to be better. I love myself more today than yesterday and treat myself as someone who is deeply loved. I am cherished by myself. I blossom with joy and beauty. Love is my nourishment that brings me to greatness. The more I love myself, the more I love others. Together we lovingly nourish an ever more beautiful world. With joy, I recognize my perfection and the perfection of Life. And so it is!

❀ ❀ ❀

🌿 Chapter Two 🌿

WISE WOMEN

---

*"I claim my feminine power now.
If I do not have Mr. Right in my life at
the moment, I can still be Ms. Right
for myself."*

(This chapter is primarily for women. But men, please remember that the more women have it together, the better life will be for *you*. Ideas that work for women also work for men. Just substitute "he" for "she"; women have been doing that for years.)

We Have a Lot to Do and a Lot to Learn

Life comes in waves and learning experiences and periods of evolution. For so long, women have been totally subjected to the whims and belief systems of men. We were told what we could do, when we could do it, and how. As a little girl, I remember I was taught to walk two steps behind a man and to look up to him and say, "What do I think, and what do I do?" I was not told to do this literally, but I watched my mother and that is what she did, so that is the behavior I learned. Her background taught her to show complete obedience to men, so she accepted abuse as normal, and so did I. This is a perfect example of **how we learn our patterns.**

It took me a long time to realize that such behavior was not normal nor was it what I, as a woman, deserved. As I slowly changed my own inner belief system, my consciousness, I began to create self-worth and self-esteem. At the same time, my world changed, and I no longer attracted men who were dominant and abusive. Inner self-esteem and self-worth are the most important things women can possess. And if we do not have these qualities, then we need to develop them. When our self-worth is strong, we will not accept positions of inferiority and abuse. We only accept that behavior because we believe we are "no good" or worthless.

No matter where we came from, no matter how abused we were as children, we can learn to love and cherish ourselves today. As women and mothers, we can teach ourselves to develop a sense of self-worth, and then we will automatically pass this trait on to our children. Our daughters will not allow themselves to be abused, and our sons will have respect for everybody, including all the women in their lives. No baby boy is born an abuser, and no baby girl is born a victim or lacking in self-worth. Abuse of others and lack of self-esteem is *learned* behavior. Children are taught violence and taught to accept victimhood. If we want the adults in our society to treat each other with respect, then we must raise the children in our society to be gentle and to have self-respect. Only in this way will the two sexes truly honor each other.

Let's Get Our Own Acts Together

Building up women does not mean having to diminish men. Male bashing is as bad as female harassment. Self-bashing is also a waste of time. We don't want to get into that. This behavior keeps us all stuck, and I feel we have had quite enough of being stuck. Blaming ourselves or men for all the ills in our lives does nothing to heal the situation, and only keeps us powerless. Blame is always a POWERLESS act. The best thing we can do for the men in our world is to stop being victims and get our own acts together. Everybody respects someone with self-esteem. We want to come from a loving space in our hearts and see everyone on this planet as someone who needs love. When women get it together, we will move mountains. And the world will be a better place in which to live.

As I mentioned earlier, this chapter is primarily for women, but men can get a lot out of it, too, as the tools that work for women also work for men. Women need to know—REALLY KNOW—that they are not second-class citizens. That is a myth perpetuated by certain segments of society—and it's nonsense. The soul has no inferiority; the soul does not even have sexuality. I know that when the feminist movement first came about, the women were so angry at the injustices that were levied upon them that they blamed the men for everything. That was okay at the time, though; these women needed to get out their frustrations for a while—sort of like therapy. You go to the therapist to work out your childhood abuse, and you NEED to express all those feelings before you can heal. When a group has been repressed for a long time, they go hog wild when they first experience their freedom.

I see Russia today as a perfect example of this phenomenon. Can you even begin to imagine living under those circumstances of extreme repression and terror for so many years, and all the repressed rage and anger that must have been building within each person? Then, suddenly, the country becomes "free," but nothing is done to heal the people. The chaos that is now going on in Russia is normal and natural considering the circumstances. These people were never taught to care for each other or love themselves. They have no role models of peace. I feel that the whole country needs deep therapy to heal the scars.

However, when people are given time to express those feelings, the pendulum swings to a more balanced point. This is what is happening to women now. It is time to release the anger and blame, the victimhood, and the powerlessness. Now it is time for women to acknowledge and claim their own power, to take their thinking in hand and to begin to create the world of equality they say they want.

When women learn to take care of themselves in a positive way, to have self-respect and self-worth, life for all human beings, including men, will have taken a quantum jump in the right direction. There will be respect and love between the sexes, and both men and women will honor each other. Everyone will have learned that there is plenty for everyone and that we can bless and prosper each other. We can all be happy and whole.

We Have the Resources to Effect Change

For a long time, women have wanted to have more dominion over their own lives. Now we have the opportunity to be all that we can be. Yes, there is still much inequity in the earning power and legal power of men and women. We still settle for what we can get in the courts of law. The LAWS were written for men. The courts talk about what a REASONABLE MAN would do, even in cases of rape.

I would like to encourage women to begin a grass roots campaign to rewrite the laws so that they are equally favorable to both men and women. Women have tremendous collective power when they get behind an issue. Remember, it is the women that elected Bill Clinton, mostly in a reaction to the treatment of Anita Hill. We need to be reminded of our power, our collective power. The combined energy of women united in a common cause is powerful indeed. Seventy-five years ago, women were campaigning for their right to vote. Today we can run for office.

We have come a long way, and we don't want to lose sight of that. Yet, we are just beginning this new phase of our evolution. We have much to do and much to learn. Women now have a new frontier of freedom—and we need creative solutions for all women, including those who live alone.

The Opportunities Are Limitless!

One hundred years ago, an unmarried woman could only be a servant in someone else's home, usually on an unpaid basis. She had no status, no say in things, and had to take life as it was handed to her. In those days—yes, it's true—a woman needed a man to have a complete life, sometimes just to survive. Even 50 years ago, the choices for an unmarried woman were narrow and limited.

Today, an unmarried American woman has the whole world in front of her. She can rise as high as her capabilities and her belief in herself. She can travel, choose her jobs, make good money, have lots of friends, and develop great self-esteem. She can even have sexual partners and loving relationships if she wants them. Today, a woman can choose to have a baby without having a husband and still be socially acceptable, as many of our well-known actresses and artists and public figures are doing. She can create her own lifestyle.

It is sad that so many women continue to moan and cry if they do not have a man by their side. We do not need to feel incomplete if we are not married or not in a relationship. When we "look" for love we are saying that we don't have it. But we all have love within us. No one can ever give us the love we can give ourselves. Once we give our love to our-selves, no one can ever take it from us. We want to stop "look-ing for love in all the wrong places." Being addicted to find-ing a partner is as unhealthy as remaining in an addictive or dysfunctional relationship. If we are addicted to finding a partner, then this addiction only reflects our feelings of lack. It is as unhealthy as any other addiction. It's another way of saying, "What's wrong with me?"

There is so much fear surrounding "being addicted to finding a partner." And so many feelings of "not being good enough." We have put so much pressure on ourselves to find a mate that far too many women settle for abusive relation-ships. We do not have to do this to ourselves!

We do not need to create pain and suffering in our own lives, nor do we need to feel acutely lonely and unhappy.

These are all choices, and we can make new choices that support and fulfill us. Granted, we have been programmed to accept limited choices. But that was the past. We want to remember that the point of power is always in the present moment, and we can begin right now to create new horizons for ourselves. See your time alone as a GIFT!

There is a Chinese proverb that says: WOMEN HOLD UP HALF THE SKY. It's time we make that true. We will not learn how, though, by whining or being angry or making ourselves the victims—giving men and the system our power. Men don't make us victims—we do that by giving them our power. The men in our lives are mirrors of what we believe about ourselves. So often we look to others to make us feel loved and connected when all they can do is mirror our own relationship with ourselves. So, we really need to improve this most important relationship in order to move forward. I would like to concentrate most of my work on helping women accept and use their power in the most positive ways.

Loving Yourself Is the Most Important Kind of Love

We all need to be very clear that THE LOVE IN OUR LIVES BEGINS WITH US. So often we look for "Mr. Right" to solve all our problems, in the form of our fathers, our boyfriends, our husbands. Now it is time to be "Ms. Right" for ourselves. And how do we do that? We begin by honestly looking at our flaws—not looking at what is wrong with us, but to see the barriers that we have put up that keeps us from being all that we can be. And without self-bashing, we can eliminate these barriers and make changes. Yes, many of those barriers are things we learned in childhood. But if we learned them once, then we can now unlearn them. We acknowledge that we are willing to learn to love ourselves. And then we develop a few guidelines:

STOP ALL CRITICISM. It is a useless act; it never accomplishes anything positive. Don't criticize yourself; lift that burden right now. Don't criticize others, either, as the faults we usually find in others are merely projections of things we don't like in ourselves. Thinking negatively about another person is one of the greatest causes of limitation in your own life. Only *we* judge ourselves—not Life, not God, not the Universe. Affirm: I LOVE AND APPROVE OF MYSELF.

DON'T SCARE YOURSELF. We all want to stop that. Too often we terrorize ourselves with our own thoughts. We can only think one thought at a time. Let's learn to think in positive affirmations. In this way our thinking will change our lives for the better. If you catch yourself scaring yourself, immediately affirm: I RELEASE MY NEED TO SCARE MYSELF. I AM A DIVINE, MAGNIFICENT EXPRESSION OF LIFE, AND I AM LIVING FULLY FROM THIS MOMENT ON.

BE COMMITTED TO THE RELATIONSHIP YOU HAVE WITH YOURSELF. We get so committed to other relationships, but we sort of toss ourselves away. We get around to ourselves only now and then. So, really care for who you are. Be committed to loving yourself. Take care of your heart and soul. Affirm: I AM MY FAVORITE PERSON.

TREAT YOURSELF AS THOUGH YOU ARE LOVED.
Respect and cherish yourself. As you love yourself, you
will be more open to love from others. The Law of
Love requires that you focus your attention on what
you *do* want, rather than on what you *don't* want. Focus
on loving YOU. Affirm: I LOVE MYSELF TOTALLY
IN THE NOW.

TAKE CARE OF YOUR BODY. Your body is a precious temple. If you are going to live a long, fulfilling
life, then you want to take care of yourself now. You
want to look good and most of all, feel good.
Nutrition and exercise are important. You want to
keep your body flexible and moving easily until your
final day on this wonderful Earth. Affirm: I AM
HEALTHY, HAPPY, AND WHOLE.

EDUCATE YOURSELF. Too often we complain that
we don't know this or that, and we don't know what to
do. But you are bright and smart, and you can learn.
There are books and classes and tapes everywhere. If
money is a consideration, then use the library. I know I
shall be learning until my very last day on this planet.
Affirm: I AM ALWAYS LEARNING AND GROWING.

BUILD A FINANCIAL FUTURE FOR YOURSELF.
Every woman has a right to have money of her own.
This is a significant belief for us to accept. It is part of
our self-worth. We can always start on a small level.
The important thing is that we keep saving.
Affirmations are important to use here, such as: I AM
CONSTANTLY INCREASING MY INCOME. I PROS-
PER WHEREVER I TURN.

FULFILL YOUR CREATIVE SIDE. Creativity can be anything that fulfills you. It could be anything from baking a pie to designing a building. Give yourself some time to express yourself. If you have children and time is short, find a friend who will help you take care of your children, and vice versa. You both deserve time for yourselves. You're worth it. Affirm: I ALWAYS FIND TIME TO BE CREATIVE.

MAKE JOY AND HAPPINESS THE CENTER OF YOUR WORLD. Joy and happiness are always within you. Make sure you are connected with it. Build your life around this joy. A good affirmation to use daily is: JOY AND HAPPINESS ARE AT THE CENTER OF MY WORLD.

DEVELOP A STRONG SPIRITUAL CONNECTION WITH LIFE. This connection may or may not have anything to do with the religion you were raised in. As a child, you had no choice. Now as an adult, you can choose your own spiritual beliefs. Solitude is one of the special times in one's life. Your relationship with your inner self is the most important. Give yourself quiet reflection time; connect with your inner guidance. Affirm: MY SPIRITUAL BELIEFS SUPPORT ME AND HELP ME BE ALL THAT I CAN BE.

You might copy the above guidelines and read them once a day for a month or two—until they are firmly in your consciousness, and they are a part of your life.

There Are So Many Types of Love

Many women will never have children in this lifetime. Don't buy into the belief that a woman is unfulfilled without a child. I always believe that there is a reason for everything. Perhaps you are meant to do other things in life. If you long for children and acutely feel this as a loss, then grieve about it. And then move on. Get on with your life. Don't sit in the grieving process forever. Affirm: I KNOW THAT EVERY-THING THAT HAPPENS IN MY LIFE IS PERFECT. I AM DEEPLY FULFILLED.

My personal belief is to stay away from fertility treatments. If your body is meant to have a baby, it will. If your body does not get pregnant, then there is a good reason. Accept it. Then get on with your life. Fertility treatments are expensive, experimental, and dangerous. We are now beginning to read about some of the horrors associated with them. One woman who had 40 treatments, at vast expense, did not get pregnant, but she did get aids. One of the many donors she used had the dis-ease.

Don't let doctors experiment with your body. When we use unnatural methods to force the body to do something that in its wisdom it does not want to do, we are asking for trouble. Don't fool around with Mother Nature. Look at all the problems many women are having because of breast implants. If your breasts are small, rejoice in them. Your body is exactly what you chose to have when you decided to incarnate this time. Be happy with who you are.

I know I have had many children in my many lifetimes. This lifetime I do not have them. I accept this as perfect for me for this time around. There are so many abandoned children in this world, if we really want to fulfill the maternal instinct, then adoption is a good alternative. We can also mother other women. Take a lost woman under your wing and help her to fly. Rescue abandoned, abused, and other homeless animals.

There are also many single mothers struggling to raise children alone. It is a very difficult job, and I applaud each and every one who goes through this experience. These women really know what *tired* means.

But remember, we don't have to be "super-women" and we don't have to be "perfect parents." If you learn some skills, read some of the great books that are out now on parenting. If you are a loving parent, your children have an excellent chance of growing up to be the sort of people you would like to have as friends. They will be individuals who are self-fulfilled and successful. Self-Fulfillment brings Inner Peace. I think the best thing we can do for our children is to learn to love ourselves, for children always learn by example. You will have a better life, and they will have a better life. (A wonderful book for parents is *What Do You Really Want for Your Children?*, by Dr. Wayne W. Dyer.)

There is also a positive side to being a single parent. Now women have an opportunity to raise their sons to be the men they say they want. Women complain so much about the behavior and attitudes of men, and yet, women raise the sons. Blame is such a waste of energy. It is another powerless act. If we want men in our lives who are kind and loving and who reveal their sensitive, feminine sides, then it is up to us to raise them that way.

If you are a single mother, above all do not bad-mouth your ex-husband. This only teaches your children that marriage is war. A mother has more influence over the child than anyone else. Mothers unite! When women get it together, we can have the kind of men we say we want in ONE generation!

Let's ask ourselves a few questions. When answered honestly, your answers can give you a new direction in life:

- How can I take this time to make my life the best it can be?

- What are the things I want from a man?

- What are the things that I believe I need to get from a man?

- What is it I can do to fill these areas? (Don't expect a man to be EVERYTHING for you. That's a terrible burden for him.)

- What would fulfill me? And how can I give it to myself?

- What is my excuse when I have no one to put me down?

- If I never had a man in my life again, would I destroy myself over that lack? (Or would I create a wonderful life and become a shining beacon for other women? That is, a way-*shower!*)

- What can I give to Life? What is my purpose? What have I come to learn? And what have I come to teach?

- How can I cooperate with Life?

Remember, the smallest positive change in your thinking can unravel the biggest problem. When you ask the right questions of Life, Life will answer.

Find Your Inner Resources

The mere question: How can I fulfill myself without a man? can be a frightening concept for many women, and we need to acknowledge our fears and to walk through those fears. Dr. Susan Jeffers wrote a whole book on this subject, *Feel the Fear and Do It Anyway.* I also highly recommend her book, *Opening Our Hearts to Men.*

Women Alone: Creating a Joyous and Fulfilling Life, is a book by Ione Jenson and Julie Keene. It explores the ever-growing options for women who are living alone. Almost every woman lives alone at some point in her life—either as a young single person, a divorced woman, or a widow. A question every bride needs to ask herself before having children, is: "Am I willing to raise my children by myself?" Similarly, all married women need to ask themselves, "Am I prepared to live by myself?"

As the authors of *Women Alone* say, "The time has come to shift our perceptions and to look at the state of 'being without a committed partner' within a larger context. As women alone, perhaps we are being called upon to be the new pioneers of a larger evolutionary purpose, and we are being asked to play a role in allowing a new model for life on our planet to emerge."

I feel that every woman is a pioneer today. Early pioneer women blazed trails. They took risks. They dealt with loneliness and fear. They lived lives of poverty and hardship. They had to help build their own shelters and forage for their own food. Even if married, their men were often away from home for long periods of time. Women had to fend for themselves and their children. They had to find their own resources. And they laid the groundwork for settling this country. Today's pioneer women are like you and me. We have incredible opportunities to fulfill ourselves and to bring about equality between the sexes. We want to bloom where we are planted!

From the level of emotional maturity, women are at their

highest point in their evolution in this lifetime. Women are now the best they have ever been. So it is time for us to shape our own destiny. There are many possibilities in life beyond what we may presently think or experience. We have opportunities never available to women before. It is time to join with *other* women to improve life for all of us. This will, in turn, improve life for men. When women are fulfilled and satisfied and happy, they will be superb partners, wonderful people to live with and work with. And men will feel infinitely more comfortable with equals. We want to bless and prosper each other.

We need to create something called *Every Woman's Guide for Successful Living.* It will not only be a woman's survival manual, but it will also create a new paradigm for women. We want to encourage every woman to be the best that she can be. If we discourage another person, that discouragement will come back to us in some way. As we give encouragement to others, Life will encourage us in very special ways. Life is very forgiving. Life simply asks us to be forgiving to ourselves, and forgiving of our neighbors.

The option of finding the "right man" is ONLY ONE alternative in a long list of possibilities. If you are single, do not put your life ON HOLD until you find a man. Get on with your life. If you don't, you might miss out on life—your *whole* life.

There's no question that men are magnificent creatures—I LOVE MEN! But women who strive to be equal with men lack ambition and originality. We don't want to be LIKE someone else; we want to be ourselves.

As Judge Lois Forer says in her wonderful book, *What Every Woman Needs to Know Before (and After) She Gets Involved with Men and Money,* "The AIM OF WOMEN is not to emulate men, but to be complete, fulfilled human beings, FEMALE human beings, persons who enjoy all the rights, privileges, and entitlements of ALL citizens of this country, and also the very special pleasures of being a woman."

We want to find our Inner Resources and our Universal Connection. We want to find and use our Inner Core. We all have a treasure trove of wisdom, peace, love, and joy inside of us. And these treasures are only a breath away. We are meant to explore new depths within ourselves. And to make new choices. We, as women, have been programmed to accept limited choices. Many married women are extremely lonely because they feel they have lost their choices. They have given their power away. They do what I used to do— they look to a man and say: "What do I think and do?" In order to have change in our lives, remember that we first need to make these new choices in our minds. We change our own thinking, and then the outer world responds differently to us.

Connect with the Treasures Within

So, I am asking you to go within and change your thinking. Connect with the treasures within you, and use them. When we connect with the treasures within, then we will give to life from the magnificence of our being. Connect with your treasures EVERY DAY.

Treat yourself special, as though you are a beloved friend. Make a date with yourself once a week and keep it. Go to a restaurant or a movie or a museum, or play a sport you particularly like. Dress up for this event. Eat from your best dishes. Wear your nicest lingerie. Don't save the good stuff for company. Be your *own* company. Allow yourself to have facials and massages; pamper yourself. If you don't have a lot of money, then trade massages or facials with a friend.

Be grateful for life. Do random acts of kindness. Pay tolls for others. In a public rest room, pick up paper towels, wipe sinks, push down paper in waste baskets, make it nice for the next person. Pick up trash on the beach or in a park. Give a flower to a stranger. Speak to a homeless person. Do a healing meditation for a gang member. Tell someone how much you appreciate him or her. Read to a lonely senior. Acts of kindness make us feel good.

* * *

We are born alone and we die alone. We choose how to fill in the spaces in between. There is no limit to our creativity. We want to find joy in our capabilities. So many of us were raised to believe we couldn't take care of ourselves. It feels GREAT to know we can. Say to yourself: WHATEVER HAPPENS, I KNOW I CAN HANDLE IT.

We want to create a rich inner space. Let your thoughts be your own best friends. Most people think the same thoughts over and over. We think on the average of 60,000 thoughts a day, and most of them are the same thoughts we had the day before and the day before that. Our thinking patterns can become ruts of negativity. Think new thoughts every day. Think creative thoughts. Think of new ways to do old things. Have a strong philosophy of Life—one that supports you in every way. Here is mine:

1. I AM ALWAYS SAFE AND DIVINELY PROTECTED.

2. EVERYTHING I NEED TO KNOW IS REVEALED TO ME.

3. EVERYTHING I NEED COMES TO ME IN THE PERFECT TIME/SPACE SEQUENCE.

4. LIFE IS A JOY AND FILLED WITH LOVE.

5. I AM LOVING AND LOVED.

6. I AM VIBRANTLY HEALTHY.

7. I PROSPER WHEREVER I TURN.

8. I AM WILLING TO CHANGE AND GROW.

9. ALL IS WELL IN MY WORLD.

I repeat these sentences often. I will say them over and over if something goes awry in any area. For instance, if I feel under the weather, then I repeat: I AM VIBRANTLY HEALTHY until I feel better. If I walk in a dark area, I will repeatedly affirm: I AM ALWAYS SAFE AND DIVINELY PROTECTED. These beliefs are so much a part of me that I can turn to them in an instant. Make a list that reflects your philosophy of life today. You can always change it or add to it. Create your personal laws now. Create a safe universe for yourself. The only power that could harm your body or your environment would be your own thoughts and beliefs. These thoughts and beliefs are changeable.

You are with the perfect partner at the moment—yourself! Before you came to the planet this time, you chose to be who you are this lifetime. Now you get to spend your whole life with you. Rejoice in this relationship. Make it the best, most loving relationship you can have. Be loving to yourself. Love the body you chose; it will be with you all your life. If there are things about your personality you would like to change, then change them. Do so with love and laughter, lots of laughter.

This is all part of our soul's evolution. I believe this is the most exciting time to be alive. I thank God every morning when I wake up for the privilege of being here and experiencing all that is. I trust my future to be GOOD.

AFFIRMATIONS FOR WOMEN

(Choose affirmations that empower you as a woman. Every day, affirm at least one of the following:)

I AM DISCOVERING HOW WONDERFUL I AM.

I SEE WITHIN MYSELF A MAGNIFICENT BEING.

I AM WISE AND BEAUTIFUL.

I LOVE WHAT I SEE IN ME.

I CHOOSE TO LOVE AND ENJOY MYSELF.

I AM MY OWN WOMAN.

I AM IN CHARGE OF MY LIFE.

I EXPAND MY CAPABILITIES.

I AM FREE TO BE ALL THAT I CAN BE.

I HAVE A GREAT LIFE.

MY LIFE IS FILLED WITH LOVE.

THE LOVE IN MY LIFE BEGINS WITH ME.

I HAVE DOMINION OVER MY LIFE.

I AM A POWERFUL WOMAN.

I AM WORTHY OF LOVE AND RESPECT.

I AM SUBJECT TO NO ONE; I AM FREE.

I AM WILLING TO LEARN NEW WAYS OF LIVING.

I STAND ON MY OWN TWO FEET.

I ACCEPT AND USE MY OWN POWER.

I AM AT PEACE BEING SINGLE.

I REJOICE IN WHERE I AM.

I LOVE AND APPRECIATE MYSELF.

I LOVE, SUPPORT, AND ENJOY THE WOMEN IN
MY LIFE.

LIFE!

I AM DEEPLY FULFILLED BY MY LIFE.

I EXPLORE ALL THE MANY AVENUES OF LOVE.

I LOVE BEING A WOMAN.

I LOVE BEING ALIVE AT THIS POINT IN TIME
AND SPACE.

I FILL MY LIFE WITH LOVE.

I ACCEPT MY GIFT OF THIS ALONE TIME.

I FEEL TOTALLY COMPLETE AND WHOLE.

I AM SAFE, AND ALL IS WELL IN MY WORLD.

I AM A POWERFUL WOMAN, INFINITELY WORTHY
OF LOVE AND RESPECT.

※　※　※

I AM NOW WILLING TO
SEE THE MAGNIFICENCE OF ME

I now choose to eliminate from my mind and life every negative, destructive, fearful idea and thought that would keep me from being the magnificent woman that I am meant to be. I now stand up on my own two feet, and support myself and think for myself. I give myself what I need. It is safe for me to grow. The more I fulfill myself, the more people love me. I join the ranks of women healing other women. I am a blessing to the planet. My future is bright and beautiful. And so it is!

※　※　※

❧ Chapter Three ❧

A HEALTHY BODY,
A HEALTHY PLANET

---

*"I take care of my body temple by fueling it
with nutritious foods and giving it lots of
exercise. I love every part of my body.
My body has always known
how to heal itself."*

A Garden of Healing

I truly feel that I am now one with all of life. I am in tune with the seasons, with the weather, the soil, the vegetation, and each and every creature that dwells on the earth and in the oceans and that flies in the air. It cannot be otherwise. We all use the same air and soil and water. We are totally interdependent upon one another.

As I work in my garden, lovingly enriching the soil, planting, harvesting, and recycling, I feel this oneness, this unity. I can take a small section of hard, unproductive earth, often filled with weeds, and slowly transform it into rich loam that will support life in all its many forms. It is like taking a portion of our mind that is filled with destructive thoughts and patterns and nourishing it so that it can create and support healthy, enriching experiences. Positive, loving thoughts produce wellness. Negative, fearful, hateful thoughts contribute to dis-ease.

We can heal our minds. We can heal our souls. We can heal our soil. We can help create a healthy planet where we can all prosper and live with joy and ease. But it is not until we love ourselves that we can accomplish this healing. People who don't respect themselves seldom respect the environment or even feel a need to care for it. It is not until we love and become in tune with nature that we can turn our earth into fertile gardens. When you see the earthworm in your garden, then you will know that you have created an environment that will support life.

The earth truly is our mother; we need her to survive. The earth does not need humanity to thrive. Long before we came to this planet, Mother Earth was doing quite nicely. If we don't have a loving relationship with her, we are goners. It is time for us to change the momentum of destruction that has been created.

In the last two centuries of so-called civilized evolution, we have done more to destroy this planet than in the preceding 2,000 centuries. In less than 200 years, more damage has been done to this planet than in the previous 200,000 years. This does not speak very highly of the stewardship that we have been entrusted with.

You cannot cut down a tree and expect there to be a continuation of the same level of oxygen supply that there was before. You cannot dump chemicals into rivers, lakes, and streams and expect to drink that water without it affecting the physical body. We and our children now get to drink this impure water. You cannot keep dumping toxins and chemicals into the atmosphere and expect the air to cleanse itself. Mother Earth is doing the best she can to combat these destructive practices of humanity.

We all need to develop an intimate relationship with the earth. Talk to her. Ask Mother Earth, "How can I cooperate with you? How can I receive your blessing and in turn bless you?" We want to love this little ball of dirt hurtling through space. It is all we have right now. If we don't take care of it, who will? Where will we live? We have no right to go to outer space when we can't even take care of our own planet.

Our earth's consciousness exists in a different time relation. It doesn't care whether humanity is here or not. The earth is a great teacher to those who take the time to listen. Life will not end here, no matter what humanity does. The earth will continue. Only humanity will return to the nothingness from whence it came unless we change our ways. Everyone in the world, no matter where you live, or how you live, has an intimate relationship with the earth. Make sure that yours is a loving, supportive one.

My Philosophy on Food

From the harvest comes the food that we prepare to nourish our bodies. Simply cooked with few ingredients, we have food fit for a healthy human body. It seems that as Americans, we have drifted away from healthful eating to the convenience of fast foods. We are the most overweight, sick nation in the Western world. We overeat fatty, processed foods that are full of chemicals. We support the food manufacturers at the expense of our own health. The five biggest selling items in supermarkets are, in order: Coca-Cola, Pepsi-Cola, Campbell's Soup, processed cheese, and beer. These items contain large amounts of sugar and/or salt. Not one of them contributes to good health.

The meat and dairy industries—not to mention the tobacco industry—have sold us a bill of goods, insisting that excessive amounts of milk and meat are good for us. However, it is precisely these massive amounts of meat and milk products that are contributing to the overwhelming incidences of breast cancer (and other cancers) and heart dis-ease in this country. The tremendous abuse and overuse of antibiotics is allowing new, never-before-heard-of dis-eases to make their way into our lives. Antibiotics kill life! The medical community admits that they have no way to handle these new dis-eases, so they turn to the wealthy pharmaceutical companies to torture animals with their product testing just to create a new chemical that will only contribute to the breakdown of our immune systems.

Genetically engineered hormones invade our milk supplies, and it has now become dangerous to our health to eat many other dairy products as well—yogurt, butter, cheese, ice cream, cream sauces, creamed soups, and anything else that is made with milk, including our beloved pancakes.

These hormones also come from the pharmaceutical companies. As a concerned human being, you need to know if the milk you buy contains genetically engineered hormones. Ask your retailer and demand an answer.

Find out if the ice cream you feed your children is slowly poisoning them. Ice cream used to be made only from whole milk, eggs, and sugar. Today, manufacturers are not required to put the many synthetic ingredients on the label.

My basic philosophy on food is: If it grows, eat it; if it does not grow, don't eat it. Fruits, vegetables, nuts, and grains grow. Twinkies and Coca-Colas do not grow. Things that grow nourish your body. Manmade, processed foods cannot sustain life. No matter how beautiful and inviting the picture on the package is, there is no life within that package!

The cells in your body are living and, as such, need living food to grow and reproduce. Life has already provided us with everything we need to feed ourselves and to remain healthy. The simpler we can eat, the healthier we will be.

We are what we think and what we eat. Knowing that whatever we give out, we always get back, I often wonder about the karma of the food manufacturers who knowingly create foods that harm the body, or of the cigarette manufacturers who put additives in their tobacco products to make them more addictive.

We need to pay attention to what we put in our bodies! Because if we don't, who will? We prevent dis-ease through conscious living. Some people see their bodies as machines to be abused and then take them to the body shop to be repaired!

My Healing Path

I was diagnosed with cancer in the mid-1970s. It was at that time that I became aware of all the negative thoughts that were swimming around in my consciousness. Unfortunately, there was also a great deal of harmful junk food lodged in my body.

In order to heal myself, I knew that it was essential that I remove both the negative beliefs that were contributing to my unhealthy physical condition, as well as the nonsupportive ways that I had been unknowingly feeding my body.

My first step was to take a holistic, metaphysical pathway to healing. I asked the medical profession for six months' time before I had to have surgery, using the excuse that it would take me that long to save the money for the operation. I then found a wonderful naturopathic doctor who taught me so much about holistic health.

He put me on a predominantly raw-food diet for six months, and I was scared enough by my cancer diagnosis to follow this diet to the letter. I ate enormous amounts of sprouts and puréed asparagus, and took colonics, had foot reflexology, and gave myself coffee enemas. I also walked a lot, prayed, and engaged in intensive therapy to release old resentment patterns from my childhood. Most importantly, I practiced forgiveness, and I learned to treasure myself. Through therapy I learned to see the truth about my parents' childhoods, and as I began to understand their backgrounds, I was able to start the forgiveness process.

I cannot say that any one thing produced a cure, but within six months, I was able to get the medical profession to agree with what I already knew: I NO LONGER HAD ANY TRACE OF CANCER!

Healthy Fuel for the Body

Since that time in my life, I have explored many different holistic systems and have found that some were more conducive to my personal lifestyle than others. I learned that I loved macrobiotic food, but that cooking in this style was too time-consuming for me. I also gained an appreciation for the raw-food program of nutritionist Ann Wigmore and others, which I found to be very cleansing and delicious. My body loves lots of raw food in the summer, but I can only eat a limited quantity in the winter, as my body tends to get too cold.

The food-combining method promoted in Harvey and Marilyn Diamond's book, *Fit for Life,* is another healthful alternative. The authors recommend eating only fruit in the morning, and then to avoid eating starches and proteins at the same meal—that is, to eat proteins with vegetables and starches with vegetables. Each group of foods needs a different enzyme for complete digestion. When starches and proteins are eaten together, the different digestive enzymes cancel each other out, and digestion only partially occurs. Not only will food combining improve your digestion, it will also help you lose weight!

Exploring many different types of systems—whatever works best for you—allows us to formulate a combination diet that is best for our own bodies.

For me, the results of my new outlook on food were apparent in my total being. When I began to learn about nutrition, I leaned toward eating healthier food. Just like when I came to a realization about the laws of Life and began to think healthier thoughts. Today, in my late sixties, I have more energy than I had 30 years go. I can work in my garden all day and lift 40-pound bags of compost. I find that if I feel sniffles coming on, I can release them quickly. If I overindulge at a party, then the next day, I know what foods to eat to bring my energy back. All in all, I lead a healthier, happier life!

Cleaning Up Your Diet

The body shifts out of balance when it is fed too many processed foods and additives. White flour and sugar contribute to ill health, as does oversprayed produce and excessive consumption of meats and dairy products, all of which burden the body with toxins. On the physical level, arthritis is a disease of toxicity; the body becomes loaded down with too much acidity. A diet that is rich in grains, vegetables, and fresh fruits is a good first step on the road to wellness.

Also, you really need to pay attention to what you eat and how you feel after you eat. For example, if you have lunch, and an hour later you want to go to sleep, then obviously something you've eaten has not agreed with you. Start keeping a record of what foods give you a lot of energy, and then eat lots of them. Keep track of the foods that bring you down, and eliminate them from your diet.

If you find that you have a lot of allergies, my first comment (on a metaphysical level), would be, "Who are you allergic to?" On the physical level, you might want to seek out a good nutritionist. If you don't know where to find a nutritionist, I would suggest you go to your local health food store. Ask the personnel there for a recommendation. They always know about the local Wellness Practitioners. What I look for when I meet a new nutritionist is someone who will give me a diet specifically tailored for my particular needs, rather than someone who just doles out a standard diet to everybody.

I find that cow's milk, which is so harmful to the body, can be substituted with soy milk, which more and more supermarkets are starting to carry. Since my body doesn't do too well with soy products, I substitute a rice milk called Rice Dream. The plain variety is great for drinking and for all types of cooking, and the vanilla and carob flavors are delicious for desserts. I often use the vanilla flavor over breakfast cereals (and sometimes even use apple juice in this way, too).

I find that fasting is also an excellent cleansing technique. One or two days on fruit or vegetable juice or potassium broth can do wonders for the body, but I think that longer fasts are advisable ONLY UNDER THE SUPERVISION OF A TRAINED PROFESSIONAL WHO IS WELL VERSED IN FASTING.

If you do decide to go on a juice fast (or you just want to make delicious juice at any time), it is great to have your own juicer. I personally like the Champion Juicer. It's big and heavy and will last a long time. It is also the only juicer that I know of that can purée frozen fruits that taste like ice cream or sherbet. It is also easy to clean. The trick to cleaning juicers is to do so immediately after usage. Rinse the juicer thoroughly BEFORE you drink your juice. If you let it stand, then the little holes get clogged and stuck, and it is very hard to clean. There are also centrifugal juicers, which work well for small batches of fruits and vegetables. However, they are harder to clean and go into overload if you are making a lot of juice.

Whenever I can, I spend one day a week in bed resting, reading, or writing on the computer. I stay in bed and eat very lightly, sometimes just liquids. The next day I feel like a new person with a lot more energy. This is an act of loving myself.

Yes, I do eat small amounts of meat now and then. Although I eat a great deal of vegetables, I am not a total vegetarian. My system does require some meat once or twice a week, but I do try to stick with New Zealand lamb or some rare, hormone-free beef or free-range veal, and occasionally chicken or fish.

I have also slowly reduced the sugar content of my foods over a period of time and now seldom use any. When cooking at home, I use a product called FRUITSOURCE, an all-purpose sweetener made from grapes and grains. I personally would never use the artificial sweeteners that you see on restaurant tables. If you read the labels on those packets, they say that their product is detrimental to your health.

Dealing with Food Cravings

Cravings for certain types of food almost always indicate an imbalance of some sort in your body. *Constant Craving: What Your Food Cravings Mean and How to Overcome Them*, a book by Doreen Virtue, Ph.D., deals with this very subject. The body is trying to make up for deficiencies when it craves something. For example, too much protein can create a craving for sweets, while a lack of magnesium will often inspire a craving for chocolate. A balanced diet filled with fresh vegetables, fruits, and grains will contribute to more balanced taste buds, and you will find that your cravings will start to diminish.

Some people find that they have a craving for fatty foods above all others. As you probably know from all the publicity that "fat grams" have been getting in the news, eating excessive amounts of fat can cause clogged arteries, heart dis-ease, and, of course, weight gain. Unfortunately, most of us were brought up on a high-fat diet when we were children, so it can be a challenge to start eating simple foods. We think the taste of fat is normal—and tasty—a double cheeseburger with a side of fries is loaded with nonsaturated fat and salt. Yet, after a three-day juice fast, simple foods taste great. So, if you find that you crave the taste and texture of fatty foods, try one of these affirmations:

I ENJOY SIMPLE, NATURAL FOODS.

FOODS THAT ARE GOOD FOR MY BODY TASTE DELICIOUS.

I LOVE BEING HEALTHY AND ENERGETIC.

The first week on a low-fat diet might be difficult, but as you continue to eat vegetables, fruit, and grains with minimal seasoning, your taste buds will start to change. Begin to modify your taste buds by using some of the salt substitutes. Veg-Sal is a product with a tiny bit of salt with lots of ground vegetable in it. Vegit and Mrs. Dash are also popular. Spike is another good one, although it does contain yeast. Even with the substitutes, it's a wise idea to train yourself to use a little bit less each day until you learn to enjoy the taste of unadulterated food. Sea Seasonings are seaweed granules and are a good way to incorporate sea vegetables into your diet.

Healing Your Food-Related Ailments

In the letters that I receive from people all over the world, there are certain food- and nutrition-related questions that keep coming up time after time. So, I'd like to share my thoughts with you on these subjects, but please remember that these are my personal opinions.

Anorexia

I believe that the contributing factor with respect to anorexia is self-hatred, pure and simple, accompanied by a total feeling of insecurity, of not feeling good enough. Sometime during the childhood years, certain people start to believe that there is something wrong with them, so they search for an excuse to explain their perceived inadequacies:

"If only I were thin enough, then I would be lovable, smarter, prettier," and so on. People dealing with anorexia need to accept the fact that there is NOTHING WRONG WITH THEM, that they are indeed lovable and, most importantly, worthy of their own love.

Bulimia

The mental cause of bulimia is very similar to that of anorexia, except that the anorexic can never be thin enough, while the bulimic must maintain his or her figure at all costs. The bulimic is stuffing down feelings and then purging them by vomiting. In both cases, there is a little child inside who desperately needs love. What both the anorexic and the bulimic need to know is that only they can give their inner child the love and acceptance it needs. Self-worth and self-esteem emanate from within and have nothing to do with our looks.

One of the best treatments for both anorexia and bulimia would be group therapy that focuses on loving the self. This is the ideal setting for discovering our false beliefs and learning that other people do indeed love and accept us as we are. When we learn to love ourselves, then we automatically tend to take care of ourselves and to learn what foods are best for our bodies. Healthy, nutritious food by itself will not convince the hurting child within that it is lovable.

Overeating

I believe that we gain weight because our bodies are toxic. We have stuffed them with the wrong kinds of foods for far too long. There is no point in going on a crash diet to lose weight, because after depriving yourself, you will just gain it all back quickly. The best decision is to go for health and to learn to eat in a healthful way. This practice alone will help release excess weight. And if you continue to eat healthful foods, the weight will stay off. (*Losing Your Pounds of Pain,* by Doreen Virtue, Ph.D., is a good book for those of you who want to break the link between abuse, stress, and overeating.)

Strict diets are a form of self-hatred. They do not reflect self-love, and they do not create permanent change. When there is true self-love, there is no need for dieting; the change happens automatically. Sondra Ray's book, *The Only Diet There Is,* teaches you how to remove negative thinking from your diet.

If you have children who eat junk food or who are over-weight, try to be a loving example yourself. Keep all junk foods out of your home, and study nutrition together. Have your children choose their own foods from a select group of positive choices. Experiment with how different foods affect each of you differently. Make your new way of eating a learn-ing experience. Let your children teach you something about nutrition every week.

With respect to overweight children, remember that you, as parents, do the shopping and control what foods come into your household. However, overweight children are usu-ally dealing with insecurity issues. Try to discern what is trou-bling your children so much that they need extra weight for protection. Are you being too hard on them? Where has communication broken down between you? With over-weight children, there is usually a lot more going on than just the overindulgence in too much food.

Of course, I have to add that the proliferation of fast-food restaurants have done tremendous damage to our children's health. Not only do we have many unhealthy, overweight children, but they also tend to grow up into adults who think that eating high-fat, non-nutritious food is the norm. No wonder we have such an overweight population. We have 56 million overweight people in this country. High-fat, high-sugar diets contribute to hyperactive kids, unruly teens, and many residents in the prison systems. We don't need diets, though; what we need is to go back to eating natural, healthful foods.

Hypoglycemia

Individuals dealing with hypoglycemia often feel over-burdened by life; they see life as something that is too much to handle. There is usually quite a bit of self-pity involved, too, with the general sentiment expressed being: "What's the use?!"

People with this condition need to eat small meals on a regular basis. They need to keep up their blood sugar in order to lift their energy levels. Sugar is the worst thing to take, however, because it sends the blood sugar level way up and then crashes it down, leaving the individual feeling devastated. Grains are really the best things to eat because they keep the blood sugar level at an even keel for a long time. Eating natural cereal for breakfast, hot or cold, without sugar, will keep your energy level up until lunch. Also, it's always wise for a hypoglycemic to carry small, nutritious snacks with him or her during the day. Raw vegetables, a few raw almonds, crackers, or a bit of soy cheese are some good choices. Dried fruit is not a good choice because it is too concentrated and too sweet. Again, a qualified nutritionist can offer you the best advice.

Nicotine Addiction

I smoked for many years, starting when I was 15. At that time, I wanted to appear sophisticated and grown up. I thought that cigarettes helped me calm my nerves, but they really just made me more nervous. They became a way for me to handle my emotional insecurity. Like most people, I became addicted, and it took me quite some time to finally quit forever.

Cigarettes are substitutes for many other things. They can be a smoke screen to keep people away, a substitute for companionship, a way to control feelings, a way to beat yourself up, or even a misguided way to control weight. No matter why a person begins to smoke, once started, smoking quickly becomes an addiction that is very hard to break. Now the tobacco companies are adding substances that make cigarettes even more addictive.

When cigarette smokers decide that they want to release this addictive habit, there are many avenues to take. This does not have to be a lonely struggle. But the smoker needs to really want to stop. If this is the case for you, then acupuncture will help release the cravings. There are also some homeopathic remedies such as Smoking Withdrawal Relief by Natra-Bio, or NICOSTOP tea by Crystal Star. Chewing on a piece of licorice root can be helpful, too. Check out your local health food store for other options.

Alternative Medicine, by The Burton Goldberg Group, recommends taking an Epsom salt bath with one-half pound of the salts. This pulls nicotine and tar from the skin. Shower afterward and then dry off with a white towel. You will be amazed to see the brownish residue on the towel from the nicotine that has been excreted by the skin.

I think it would be an excellent idea for everyone, smokers or not, to write to all the cigarette companies and demand that they stop putting addictive additives in the tobacco in cigarettes. This is a very wicked practice and an expression of greed at the expense of the consumer's health. If the government won't stop it, then we, the people, must.

Colds and Fevers

Metaphysically, colds relate to mental congestion. When there's too much confusion and too many projects going on, then there is often an inability to make clear decisions.

On the physical level, colds stem from putting too many un-natural foods into the body, which overcongests the bowels. Many people say, "Feed a cold and starve a fever," but what's actually being said is: "IF you feed a cold, THEN YOU WILL HAVE TO starve a fever." So, the answer is to lighten up. Lighten up your diet by eating more fresh vegetables, fruits, and grains. Leave the processed foods and heavy meats alone. And definitely take it easy on the dairy products. Milk creates mucus in the body. Lots of ear problems are aggravated by dairy products, as are lung conditions.

A cold is also nature's warning that the body needs a rest—a rest from stress and a rest from food. If we rush to the drug store to buy the latest over-the-counter medication to stifle our symptoms, then we are not allowing the healing intelligence of the body to take over. We must listen to our bodies and cooperate with their messages. Our bodies love us and want us to be healthy.

I cringe every time I see an ad on TV for the latest medication that will get you back to work in no time. When we take these formulas, it is as though we are whipping a tired horse to make it work harder. It doesn't work, and it is a very unloving act. Bodies that are mistreated give out far too soon.

Fevers usually represent burning up in anger. On the physical level, the body creates a fever to burn up the toxins. It is a way of cleaning house.

For a long time we have repressed our thoughts and emotions so fully, particularly with the use of medications, that rarely do we really know what we are thinking or feeling. We don't know if we are sick or well.

Candida

People who have candida are often very frustrated and angry and may feel scattered in their personal and professional lives. Since they are basically untrusting, they are often very demanding in relationships. They are great takers, but not very good givers. Early in life, they learned that they could not trust people who were close to them. Now, they cannot trust themselves.

According to *Healthy Healing*, an alternative healing reference by naturopathic doctor Linda Rector-Page, "Candidiasis is a state of inner imbalance, not a germ, bug, or dis-ease. Candida albicans is a strain of yeasts commonly found in the gastrointestinal and genito-urinary areas of the body. It is generally harmless, but when resistance and immunity are low, the yeast is able to multiply rapidly, feeding on sugars and carbohydrates in these tracts. It releases toxins into the bloodstream, and causes far-reaching problems. Stress and lack of rest aggravate this condition in a body that is already out of balance." *Healthy Healing* is an excellent book that I highly recommend, along with its companion book, *Cooking for Healthy Healing.*

To treat candida, nutritionists recommend eliminating

sugar, artificial sweeteners, breads, yeasts, dairy products, fruit, tea, coffee, vinegars, and tobacco, among other items, for at least two months. Candida is a condition that really requires treatment by a qualified nutritionist.

Menopause

I believe that menopause is a normal, natural process of life. It is not meant to be a dis-ease. Each month during menstruation, the body sloughs off the bed that was prepared for a baby that was not conceived. It also releases many toxins at that time. If we eat a junk-food diet or even just the standard American diet of processed foods, 20 percent sugars, and 37 percent fat, we are building up toxins all the time. Perhaps more than we can eliminate.

If we have a lot of toxins in our bodies when we are on the brink of menopause, then the process will be more uncomfortable. So, the better you take care of your body on a daily basis, the easier your menopause time will be. A difficult or easy menopause period begins with how we feel about ourselves from puberty on. Women who are experiencing a difficult menopause are usually people who have eaten poorly for a long time and who have poor mental self-images.

In the 1900s, our life spans were about 49 years. In those days, menopause was no big deal. By the time you had menopause, you were on your way out. Today our life spans are around 80 years, and menopause is an issue that must be dealt with. More and more women today are choosing to take a more active, responsible role in their health care, to grow more in harmony with their bodies, and to allow processes of change such as menopause to unfold naturally for them, with little discomfort or diminished capacities.

Like everything else in our lives, we all experience different degrees of readiness and willingness. For many of us, the level of responsibility and commitment necessary to bring our minds and bodies into harmony when it comes to deep-seated issues is too great. We need help from the medical profession or other sources until we feel ready or safe enough to confront some of the issues impacting our health and well-being, such as beliefs about self-worth. A far too common belief, in our patriarchal society, is that women have little or no worth without their reproductive powers. Is it any wonder that many women fear and resist menopause? Estrogen therapy does not address these types of issues. Only our hearts and minds can heal these perceptions.

I do feel that it is imperative that women educate themselves about what their real choices are. Please read and share with your friends the book, *THE MENOPAUSE INDUSTRY: How the Medical Establishment Exploits Women,* by Sandra Coney (Hunter House). This book points out that until the 1960s, doctors were not much interested in menopause. Women were told that it was all in their heads. After all, Freud said that menopause was a neurotic condition.

Dr. Robert A. Wilson, a New York gynecologist, founded a private trust that was supported by donations from the pharmaceutical industry. His book, *Feminine Forever,* published in 1966, launched a crusade to rescue women from the "living decay" of menopause and to have women take estrogen from puberty to grave. Today, menopause has become a commodity that can be exploited for commercial gain. The pharmaceutical industry has promoted the idea of menopause as a dis-ease because it has the drugs to treat it.

The author continues to say, "There is no area that demonstrates the entrenched sexism of medicine more sharply than that of menopause. The new view of menopause as dis-ease is socially controlling. Modern medicine does not make women more powerful and in control of their lives. They make patients out of well women."

I am not suggesting that there are not some women who are helped by Hormone Replacement Therapy (HRT). But for many in the medical establishment to now make the blanket statement that all women need HRT from menopause until death is to condemn and belittle the mid-life woman. Essentially, what I am suggesting is that striving for harmony and balance in our bodies and our minds can make potentially debilitating side effect-ridden drug therapies unnecessary.

In my own case, when I had my first hot flash I went to a friend who practiced homeopathy. He gave me one dose of a homeopathic remedy, and I never had a hot flash again. It was a blessing that he knew me so well. There are many herbs used today by nutritionists that are very helpful when you are going through this time of life. There are also natural substances that take the place of estrogen. Speak to your nutritionist about these matters.

Remember, women today are pioneers who are working to change old, negative belief patterns so that our daughters and our daughters' daughters will never have to suffer during menopause.

Water

Pure clean water. Oxygen is number one, and water is number two when it comes to the most important contributors to health. There is nothing like it. Not only does water quench thirst, but it cleanses the body. If every time you wanted a snack, you would reach for a large glass of water, you would do your body a good deed. Our bodies are almost

75 percent water. Every cell needs water to do its best work. I suggest that you learn to drink lots of water, with one exception: Do not drink water with your meals, as it will dilute your digestive fluids, and you will not get as much nourishment from your food.

Unfortunately, humankind—mostly industry—has been polluting this precious substance for some time now. Most of our municipal water is not fit to drink, being treated with many chemicals. As a result, so many of us turn to the bottled waters. Most supermarkets and even convenience stores now carry bottled water. I personally like to buy Artesian well water when I am traveling. At home I have put a water filter on the outside of my whole house, so that all the water is filtered, including the water in my shower. In the kitchen sink, I have another filter so that my drinking water is double filtered. I like the Multi-Pure Water Filters the best.

Here in Southern California, we have periodic drought seasons. During the last drought, I sent these ideas to our local newspaper:

USE COMMON SENSE TO SAVE MORE WATER

Our water has flowed so freely for so long and we have used it so lavishly, that now in this time of an intense water crisis when we are being asked to cut our individual usage by 50 percent, we do not know what to do. So here are some "common sense" guidelines that, with a little effort, we can easily follow.

1. Use every bit of water twice if you can. Don't let water run down the sink. Collect it and reuse it.
2. Wash salad greens and vegetables in a bowl. Reuse that water for house plants.

3. When you change the dog's water dish, give the water to a plant.

4. Switch to "biodegradable, non-toxic" soaps and cleansers so that you can easily reuse the water for plants without harming them. Shaklee and Amway have been making them for years. Look for other brands, too.

5. Let the dishwasher take a vacation, and go back to doing dishes by hand. You'll save water and electricity. Use one basin for washing and one for rinsing. Definitely save the rinse water.

6. All water from a vase of flowers can be reused for house plants. (They love it; the water is full of nutrients.)

7. When you brush your teeth or wash your face, again put a bowl in the sink and collect that water for outdoor plants.

8. I keep a large garbage can or two by the kitchen door and one by my bathroom door, and any water that I do not need to use at the moment, I store—dishwater, bath water, rinse water, etc.

9. Get a dam for your toilet, or make one from a double plastic bag filled with water and tied securely. In Santa Barbara, where they have been dealing with a water shortage for a long time, they have a saying, "If it's yellow, let it mellow. If it's brown, flush it down." In other words, you don't have to flush every time you use the toilet.

10. Install a "soap saver" shower head. Wet down your body, press the knob to turn off the water while you soap up, then rinse off quickly.

11. Get a flat tub stopper for the shower stall, and collect the water. Scoop it into a pail and use it for plants.

12. It may not be what you are used to, but you can easily bathe in three inches of water. Collect the bath water and reuse it in the garden. Even if you don't have a garden yourself, you could take a bucket of water outside every day and perhaps save a tree in your apartment complex. Adopt a tree somewhere, and water it regularly with water that you would otherwise let go down the drain.

13. Make sure you have a full load before you use the washer.

14. Have a tank attached to your rain gutters so that you can collect that water when it does rain.

15. Look into "gray water," water that you recycle. Have a plumber adjust your pipes so that kitchen, bath, and washing machine water all flow into the garden.

16. Enlist the children. Have a contest in your family. See who can save the most water in one day.

17. Mulch the plants you do water in the garden so that they can live on less.

Still, with all of these methods, some of the garden may have to go. Remember, it is only a temporary measure. When the rains come again, we can replant.

Also remember that in many places on the planet, they still carry water in a bucket from a central well for all household needs. As difficult as it may be to cut back now, be grateful for the convenient ways that water flows into your life. Bless the water with love each time you use it. Be thankful for all that you have.

The Joys of Exercise

Exercise is great for the body. Do anything that makes you feel good. It doesn't matter if it's bicycling, tennis, jogging, volleyball, swimming, golf, brisk walking, using a trampoline, jumping rope, playing with the dog, or whatever. Some sort of exercise is vital to maintaining optimum health. If we don't exercise at all, then the bones weaken; they require exercise to stay strong. We are living longer all the time, and we want to be able to run and jump and move easily until our last day.

I go to the gym twice a week and also do quite a bit of gardening, which is hard physical labor and keeps the body strong. Over my lifetime, I have done many sorts of exercise: Jazzercise, aerobics, matwork, yoga, trapeze work, and dance. For some time now, I've been going to a Pilates gym. We work with springs rather than weights, so the muscles stay long. This form of workout suits my body very well. I also walk fairly regularly, which I enjoy very much because it gives me a chance to take in the beautiful surroundings in my lovely Southern California neighborhood.

If you are thinking of embarking on an exercise program, start slowly, maybe with just a walk around the block after dinner. As you build your stamina, you might increase your rate and distance until you are walking at a brisk pace for a mile or more. You'll be surprised by the changes you see in your body and mind when you start taking care of yourself in this manner. Remember: Every single thing that you do for yourself is an act of self-love, or self-hate. Exercise is self-love. And loving the self is the key to success in just about every aspect of your life.

Healthy Healing has a "one-minute exercise" for those who say they have no time, or when we are too rushed to do a longer set. Simply lie flat on the floor. Then stand up in any way you can. Then lie down again. Do this for one minute. It exercises the muscles, lungs, and the circulatory system.

The Power of 5, by Harold Bloomfield, M.D., and Robert K. Cooper, Ph.D., includes many two- to five-minute exercises that you can do throughout the day. For instance, to tighten your lower abdominal area: slowly exhale and, as you reach the place where you normally finish breathing out, smoothly and forcefully breathe out *more*, using the power of your lower abdominal muscles. Work up to doing ten of these exercises each day. Fit them in wherever you can, doing one or two at a time.

My favorite "one-minute" exercise that I do when I am in a hurry is just to jump up and down 100 times. It is quick and easy and it feels good.

So you see, there are lots of ways to make sure the body doesn't get rusty and rigid. Keep moving and have fun.

To Sun or Not to Sun

I know that there is a lot of controversy about the sun these days. Yet, the natural way to receive vitamin D is to absorb it through the skin when we are out in the sunlight. Yes, I agree that to bake your body for hours and hours is not the wise thing to do. However, human beings have been on this planet for millions of years, and so has the sun. God set it up so that our bodies are compatible with the sun. In areas where the sun is very strong, nature has given us darker skin pigment. Native Africans are out in the sun all day, and they do not develop skin cancer. Unfortunately, in our modern society, we have gotten so far away from the natural-foods diet that Nature has put here for us that our bodies are out of whack on all levels, including our relationship with the sun.

We also have a thinning of the ozone level around the planet due to the extreme pollution that mankind has created. Instead of correcting the problem and treating our air as the precious commodity that it is, we have once again turned to the pharmaceutical industry for the answers, and they have created sunscreen lotions and sunblock creams. Now we are told that we must apply these chemical lotions whenever we go outside. We are even cautioned to put these unnatural substances on our children and babies. I personally believe this whole business is a big ripoff, a propaganda campaign that benefits the pharmaceutical companies.

Alternative Healing reports new research that suggests that sunscreens themselves may be instrumental in causing melanoma because they prevent the skin from producing vitamin D. There is no evidence that sunscreens prevent cancer in humans; they only prevent sunburn. The research also states that the rise in melanoma rates have been directly proportionate to the increased sale and use of sunscreens. Queensland, Australia, has the highest rate of melanoma in the world, and was also the place where sunscreens were first and most strongly recommended by the medical community.

Be sensible about your time in the sun. Overexposure to the sun increases aging of the skin, so don't overdo it. Also, be careful about which chemicals you put on your skin, because the skin absorbs them all.

Love Your Body

When you listen with love to your body's messages, you will fuel it with the food it needs, exercise it, and love it. I believe we contribute to every so-called dis-ease in our body. The body, like everything else in life, is a mirror of your inner thoughts and beliefs. The body is always talking to you, if you will take the time to listen. Every cell within your body responds to every single thought you think and every word you speak.

It's an act of love to take care of your body. As you learn more and more about nutrition, you'll start to notice how you feel after you eat certain foods. You'll figure out which foods give you optimum strength and lots of energy. Then, you'll stick to eating those foods.

I don't believe that we all have to get sick and wind up in nursing homes—that's not how we're meant to leave this extraordinary planet. I think we can take care of ourselves and be healthy for a long time.

We need to cherish and revere these wonderful temples that we live in. One way to do so is to stay away from aluminum, which is really creating so many problems. Researchers are finding out that it has a direct correlation with Alzheimer's Dis-ease. Remember that aluminum is not only in deodorants, beer, and soft drink cans, but in aluminum foil and pots and pans, which you might consider disposing of. I understand that it's also an ingredient in those spray breath fresheners and in many cake mixes. All of that stuff is just poison for your body. And why would you want to put poison in the body you love?

I believe the best way to be good to your body is to remember to love it. Look into your own eyes in the mirror often. Tell yourself how wonderful you are. Give yourself a positive message every time you see your own reflection. Just love yourself. Don't wait until you become thin or build your muscles or lower your cholesterol or reduce your fat ratio. Just do it now. Because you deserve to feel wonderful all of the time.

YOU ARE GREAT!

AFFIRMATIONS FOR LOVING THE BODY

I LOVE MY BODY.

MY BODY LOVES TO BE HEALTHY.

MY HEART IS THE CENTER OF LOVE.

MY BLOOD HAS LIFE AND VITALITY.

EVERY CELL IN MY BODY IS LOVED.

ALL OF MY ORGANS WORK PERFECTLY.

I SEE WITH LOVE.

I HEAR WITH COMPASSION.

I MOVE EASILY AND COMFORTABLY.

MY FEET DANCE THROUGH LIFE.

I BLESS MY FOOD WITH LOVE.

WATER IS MY FAVORITE BEVERAGE.

I KNOW HOW TO TAKE CARE OF MYSELF.

I AM HEALTHIER THAN I HAVE EVER BEEN.

I APPRECIATE MY GLORIOUS BODY.

❧   ❧   ❧

I AM HEALTHY, HEALED, AND WHOLE

I forgive myself for not treating my body well in the past. I was doing the best I could with the understanding and knowledge I had. Now I care enough for myself to nourish myself with all the best that Life has to offer. I give my body what it needs on every level to bring it up to optimum health. I eat nutritious foods with joy. I drink lots of nature's pure water. I continually find new ways to exercise that are fun. I love every part of my body, inside and out. I now choose the peaceful, harmonious, loving thoughts that create an internal atmosphere of harmony for the cells in my body to live in. I am in harmony with every part of life. My body is a good friend that I take loving care of. I am nurtured and nourished. I rest well. I sleep peacefully. I awaken with joy. Life is good, and I enjoy living it. And so it is!

❧   ❧   ❧

❧ Chapter Four ❧

THE RELATIONSHIPS
IN YOUR LIFE

---

*"Every person I meet is a mirror
of some part of me."*

The Most Important Relationship of All

The most lasting relationship I will ever have is the relationship I have with myself. All other relationships come and go. Even marriages that last "until death do us part," end eventually. The one person I am with forever is me. My relationship with me is eternal. So what is this relationship like? Do I wake up in the morning glad to find myself here? Am I a person I like to be with? Do I enjoy my own thoughts? Do I laugh with myself? Do I love my body? Am I content being with me?

If I don't have a good relationship with myself, how can I have a good one with someone else? If I don't love myself, I will always be looking for someone to complete me, to make me happy, to fulfill my dreams.

Attracting Healthy Relationships

Being "needy" is the best way to attract an unsuccessful relationship. As author Dr. Wayne Dyer says: "In any relationship in which two people become one, the end result is two half people." If you expect the other person to "fix" your life, or be your "better half," you are setting yourself up for failure. You want to really be happy with who you are before you enter a relationship. You want to be happy enough so that you don't even need a relationship to be happy.

Similarly, if you have a relationship with someone who does not love himself or herself, then it is impossible to really please that person. You will never be "good enough" for someone who is insecure, frustrated, jealous, self-loathing, or resentful. Too often we knock ourselves out trying to be good enough for partners who don't have any idea how to accept our love—because they don't love who they are. Life is a mirror. What we attract always mirrors those qualities we have, or beliefs we have about ourselves and relationships. What others feel about us is their own limited perspective of life. We must learn that Life has always loved us unconditionally.

Jealous people are very insecure; they don't value themselves. They have no faith in their self-worth. Jealousy is really saying, "I'm not good enough, I'm not worth loving, so I know my partner is going to cheat on me or leave me for someone else." This creates anger and blame. If you stay with a jealous person, then you are saying that you don't deserve a loving relationship.

It is often the same thing with spousal abusers. They either grow up in a family where abuse was normal and they just continue the family pattern, or they blame the world and their partners for their own lack of self-worth. Abusers will never stop the abuse pattern unless they undergo therapy. Abusers almost always have a parent they have deep resentment towards. Forgiveness is a vital issue for them. They must understand their patterns and be willing to change.

Our Parents' Influence

All my relationships are based upon the relationships I had with my parents. I was so shocked when I first discovered this. Years ago I had gone to a "Loving Relationships Workshop" conducted by Sondra Ray, expecting to learn how to attract a loving relationship. I was so dismayed when I learned that we were going to work on our relationships with our parents. By the end of the workshop, though, I learned that the reason I had so many problems in my personal relationships was because of the very difficult childhood I had.

The abuses my mother and I had endured, the abandonment and lovelessness of my childhood—it had all transferred itself into my current relationships. No wonder I attracted abusive men, no wonder they always abandoned me, no wonder I always felt unloved and unwanted, no wonder I always seemed to have bosses that frightened me. I was just living out what I had learned as a child. That was a very important workshop for me. I released a great deal of resentment and learned to work on forgiveness. The relationship with myself improved enormously. Never again did I attract an abusive man.

So, rather than wasting time saying, "Men are no good," or "Women are no good," let us look into the relationships we had with our parents or that our parents had between each other.

For example, what are your current complaints about the men or women in your life? Think about how you would fill in the blanks below.

He never _____.

He always _____.

She never _____.

She always _____.

Men won't _____.

Women won't _____.

Is this the way your mother or father behaved toward you? Did your mother treat your father this way? Or does this describe the way your father treated your mother? How was love expressed in your home when you were a child?

You may have to reach back into your childhood relationship with your father or mother to resolve deep-seated fears surrounding a relationship. Ask yourself: What do I have to give up to be in a relationship? How do I lose *me* when I am in a relationship? What messages did I receive as a child that created a belief in me that relationships are painful?

Affirm the Love for Yourself

Perhaps you have a very difficult time setting limits, and people tend to take advantage of you. You may be sending out a message that says: "I do not value and respect myself. It's okay to abuse me and take advantage of me." But this does not have to be true for you any longer. Begin today to affirm your love and respect for yourself. Look into a mirror frequently and tell yourself: I LOVE YOU. As simple as this sounds, it is a very powerful healing affirmation. As you grow in self-love, your relationships will begin to reflect this love and respect as well.

You may wish to consider joining a support group such as Co-dependents Anonymous or Al-Anon. These arc wonderful groups that will assist you in establishing boundaries in your relationships and help you reconnect with the self-love and respect that is within you. Check your local phone directory for a group near you.

It pleases me to notice that self-help groups are becoming the new social norm—people getting together with similar problems, working on solutions. If you meet someone at one of these groups, you know that while they may have some problems, they are working to improve the quality of their lives.

I believe that we have comfort zones in our relationships

with others. These comfort zones form when we are very small. If our parents treated us with love and respect, then we associate this type of treatment with being loved. If, as is the case for many of us, our parents were unable to treat us with love and respect, then we learn to be comfortable with this lack. In an effort to get our needs met, to feel loved and cared for, we associate being treated badly with being loved. This becomes our pattern, and as a pattern formed in childhood, it becomes the pattern we use unconsciously in all our relationships.

This belief pattern, that being treated badly equals love, knows no gender bias. I believe this type of dysfunctional pattern is more widely recognized in women, because culturally, women are encouraged to express vulnerability, and are thus more willing to admit when their lives are not working. This is changing, however, as more and more men become willing to reconnect with their vulnerability. *Women Who Love Too Much,* by Robin Norwood, is an excellent relationship book; and I also recommend the audiocassette album, *Making Relationships Work,* by Barbara De Angelis, Ph.D. An affirmation for all of us is: I OPEN MY HEART TO LOVE, AND I AM SAFE.

All of the important work we do is on ourselves. Wanting your mate to change is a subtle form of manipulation, a desire to have power over him or her. It may even be self-righteousness, because it is saying that you are better than he or she is. Allow your partners in life to be as they choose to be. Encourage their self-exploration, self-discovery, self-love, self-acceptance, and self-worth.

Finding Love

If you are looking for a mate, I suggest that you make a list of all the qualities you would like this person to have. Do go beyond "tall, dark, and handsome" or "cute, blonde, and pretty." List *all* the qualities you want. Then review this list and see how many of these qualities *you* possess. Are you willing to develop the ones you don't have? Then, also ask yourself what it is within you that could be denying or delaying the attraction of this person to you. Are you willing to change those beliefs?

Is there still a part of you that believes you are unlovable or unworthy of love? Is there a habit or belief you have that pushes love away? Is there a part of you that says, "I don't ever want to have a marriage like my parents; therefore, I won't fall in love"?

Perhaps you have feelings of isolation. It is very difficult to feel connected to others when, for the most part, we are disconnected from our own selves. In this case, you need to really focus some quality time on yourself right now. Become your own best friend. Rediscover what makes you happy, what you love to do; pamper and spoil yourself. So often we look to others to make us feel loved and connected, when all they can do is mirror our own relationship with ourselves.

What do you think you deserve in an intimate relationship? When we are coming from a place of feeling, we can never get what we really want; it usually means our belief system supports "not deserving." Is this what you truly believe about yourself, that you can't have what you truly want? This particular mental pattern no longer needs to be true for you. You can begin to make a change today.

Make a few lists such as: What I Believe About Men; Women; Love; Marriage; Commitment; Fidelity; Trust; and

Children. These lists will show you any negative beliefs you need to change. You may be surprised by some of the messages that are hidden in your consciousness. Clean them out, and you may be delighted to see how different your next relationship is.

It's interesting to note that most psychics report that the majority of people who come to them ask at least one of three questions. Psychics hear these same questions over and over: How can I get a relationship? How can I get rid of a relationship? How can I increase my finances?

If you are in a relationship that you really want to get out of, use that all-powerful tool: Blessing with Love. Affirm: I BLESS YOU WITH LOVE, AND I RELEASE YOU. YOU ARE FREE AND I AM FREE. Repeat this often. Then be really clear on what you *do* want in a relationship. Make a list if you need to. In the meantime, work on loving yourself nonstop. Love and accept the other person completely, just as they are. As you change and grow inside, you will find that one of two things happens automatically. The other person will either align with your desires, or they will disappear altogether. If they leave your life, this transition will be smooth. Always begin by loving and appreciating yourself...everything else will change. Use the affirmation: I NOW DISCOVER HOW WONDERFUL I AM. I CHOOSE TO LOVE AND ENJOY MYSELF.

It is very important to clean up and resolve old relationships in order to commit to a new one. If you are always talking about or thinking of your last love, you are not yet free and clear to enter the new one. Sometimes we deify our previous love in order to protect ourselves from being vulnerable in the present moment. In her book, *A Return to Love*, Marianne Williamson shares this wonderful barometer for our choices. She states that in all of our interactions, we are either "moving towards love or moving away from love." Ideally, to be fully alive and happy, we want to be making choices in our life that move us toward love.

As you work on resolving the blocks that stand between you and your relationship, practice being your own lover. Treat yourself to romance and love. Demonstrate to yourself how special you are. Pamper yourself. Treat yourself to small acts of kindness and appreciation. Buy yourself flowers, surround yourself with colors, textures, and scents that please you. Life always mirrors back to us the feeling we have inside. As your inner sense of love and romance grows, the right person to share in your increasing sense of intimacy will be attracted to you like a magnet. Most importantly, you will not have to give up any part of your own self-intimacy to be with that person.

The End of a Relationship

The end of an affair is often a very painful time. We go into the "I'm not good enough" routine and punish ourselves. We think that because the other person no longer wants to be with us, there must be something wrong with us, and we often fall into deep despair. It is not true that there is something wrong with us, though. All relationships are learning experiences. We come together for a period of time. We share energy and experiences for as long as we can. We learn what we can together. Then there comes a time to part. This is normal and natural.

Don't cling to an outworn romantic relationship just to avoid the pain of parting. Don't put up with physical or emotional abuse just to be with someone. You will never have a fulfilling life if you cling to old experiences. When we allow ourselves to be treated with disrespect, we are saying, "I am not worth loving so I have to stay here and accept this behavior. I can't bear to be alone (with just myself), and I know that I'll never find another relationship." These negative affirmations pull you down. Instead, listen to the signals.

When a relationship ends, Life is giving you a chance for a new experience. This can be a time for deep gratitude, of acknowledging the good times you had together, and of appreciating all the learning experiences. Then, you can release that relationship with love and get on with the next step in your life. This is a time for loving yourself with tenderness and understanding. This is not the end of your world; it is the beginning of a new phase. With love for yourself, this new time of your life can be far more wonderful than what you are just ending.

AFFIRMATIONS FOR THE RELATIONSHIPS IN YOUR LIFE

I HAVE COME HERE TO LEARN THAT THERE IS ONLY LOVE.

I AM DISCOVERING HOW WONDERFUL I AM. I CHOOSE TO LOVE AND ENJOY MYSELF.

AS A MAGNIFICENT CREATION OF A LOVING GOD, I AM INFINITELY LOVED, AND I ACCEPT THIS LOVE NOW.

I AM OPEN AND RECEPTIVE TO A WONDERFUL, LOVING RELATIONSHIP.

BY THINKING LOVING, SUPPORTIVE THOUGHTS, I CREATE A LOVING, SUPPORTIVE RELA-TIONSHIP.

I OPEN MY HEART TO LOVE.

IT IS SAFE FOR ME TO EXPRESS LOVE.

I GET ALONG WITH EVERYONE.

WHEREVER I AM, THERE IS JOY AND LAUGHTER.

I RELATE FROM MY HEART.

PEOPLE LOVE ME, AND I LOVE PEOPLE.

I AM IN HARMONY WITH LIFE.

I ALWAYS HAVE THE PERFECT PARTNER IN MY LIFE.

I AM SAFE AND SECURE IN MY LOVE FOR MYSELF.

I AM IN A HARMONIOUS RELATIONSHIP WITH LIFE.

❧ ❧ ❧

LIFE LOVES ME AND I AM SAFE

I envelop everyone in my life in a circle of love, no matter if they are male or female. I include my friends, my loved ones, my co-workers, and everyone from my past. I affirm that I have wonderful, harmonious relationships with everyone, where there is mutual respect and caring on both sides. I live with dignity and peace and joy. I expand my circle of love to envelop the entire planet, and this love comes back to me multiplied. Within me is unconditional love, and I express it to everyone. My unconditional love includes me, for I know I am worth loving. I love and appreciate myself. And so it is!

❧ ❧ ❧

🌿 Chapter Five 🌿

LOVE YOUR WORK

"I enjoy all the work that I do."

My Early Work Life

When I first left home, I heard about a soda-fountain job in a drug store. I remember the boss telling me how hard the work was and how there was a lot of cleaning up to do. He asked me if I thought I could handle it. Of course I said yes because I really wanted to work. At the end of the first day, I remember thinking, He thinks this is hard work? This is nothing compared to the work I did every day at home.

That job lasted two weeks because my parents found me and made me go home. My boss was sorry to see me go because I was such a good worker. When I next went out into the job market, I stepped up in the world—becoming a waitress in a small cafe. There were several other waitresses there, and on the first day, they had me cleaning the dishes from the counter. I was so naive and unworldly that I thought the tips were for me, and I put them into my pocket. By the end of the day, the other waitresses caught on and confronted me, demanding their tips. I was so embarrassed. It certainly was not the way to begin a new job. That position didn't last long either.

At that time in my life, I was so unsophisticated that I had no social graces at all. I did not know how to behave in society. My first experience going to a small restaurant was so frightening to me that I ran out in hysterics. At home I learned how to work hard, but I was not taught anything about the outside world.

Between my ignorance and my lack of self-esteem, I went through a long series of low-paying jobs. I worked in drug stores, dime stores, and in the stock room of department stores. While my dream was to be a movie star or a dancer, I had no idea how to go about achieving that. Any job beyond where I was, was a far-off dream. I was so uneducated that even a secretary's job was far beyond me.

Then one day, Life took an interesting turn; I must have been ready. I had a job in Chicago that paid $28 a week. Why I walked into the Arthur Murray dance studios one day, I cannot remember. But I did, and some slick salesperson sold me $500 worth of dance lessons. When I got home that night, I could not believe what I had done. I was terrified. The next day after work I went back to the studio and confessed my poverty. They said, "Oh, but you've signed a contract, and you must pay us the money. However, we have a position open for a receptionist. Do you think you could do that?"

The job paid ten dollars a week more than I was making. It was a large studio, with over 40 teachers. We worked 10:00 to 10:00 and always ate our meals together. Within two days, I discovered I was capable of handling the teachers' appointments, taking in money, and making all those introductions. I had a built-in social life and had never had more fun at a job. It was a great turning point in my life.

After the job at Arthur Murray, I moved to New York and became a fashion model. But I never really possessed self-worth or self-esteem until I began working on myself to release my old negative beliefs from childhood. In the early days, I had no idea how to change my situation. Now I know that the inner work must be done first. No matter how stuck we seem to be, it is always possible to make positive changes.

Bless Your Work with Love

Maybe you are in a job now where you feel stuck, or you hate it, or you find that you are just putting in your time to bring home a paycheck. Well, there are definitely things you can do to make positive changes. These ideas may sound silly or simplistic, but I know that they work. I have seen countless people change their working situations for the better.

The most powerful tool you can use to transform a situation is the power of *blessing with love*. No matter where you work or how you feel about the place, BLESS IT WITH LOVE! I mean that literally. Say, "I BLESS MY JOB WITH LOVE."

Don't stop there. Bless with love: the building, the equipment in the building, your desk if you have one, the counter if you work at one, the various machines you may use, the products, the customers, the people you work with, and the people you work for, and anything else associated with this job. It will work wonders.

If there is a person at work you are having difficulty with, then use your mind to change the situation. Use the affirmation: I HAVE A WONDERFUL WORKING RELATIONSHIP WITH EVERYONE AT WORK, INCLUDING_____. Every time that person comes into your mind, repeat the affirmation. You will be amazed by how that situation changes for the better. A solution may come about that you cannot even imagine at the moment. Speak your words, and then let the Universe figure out how to handle things.

If you want to secure a new job, then in addition to blessing your current job with love, add the affirmation: I RELEASE THIS JOB WITH LOVE TO THE NEXT PERSON, WHO WILL BE SO GLAD TO BE HERE. That job was ideal for you at the time you got it. It was the perfect reflection of your sense of self-worth at that time. Now you have grown and are moving on to better things. Now your affirmation is: I KNOW THERE ARE PEOPLE OUT THERE LOOKING FOR EXACTLY WHAT I HAVE TO OFFER. I NOW ACCEPT A JOB THAT USES ALL MY CREATIVE TALENTS AND ABILITIES. THIS JOB IS DEEPLY FUL-FILLING, AND IT IS A JOY FOR ME TO GO TO WORK EACH DAY. I WORK WITH AND FOR PEOPLE WHO APPRECIATE ME. THE BUILDING IS LIGHT, BRIGHT, AND AIRY AND FILLED WITH A FEELING OF ENTHUSI-ASM. IT IS IN THE PERFECT LOCATION, AND I EARN GOOD MONEY, FOR WHICH I AM DEEPLY GRATEFUL.

If you hate the job you have now, you will take that feeling of hatred with you. Even if you get a good new job, in a short time you will find yourself hating the new one, too. Whatever feelings you have within you now, you will carry to the new place. If you now live in a world of discontentment, you will find it everywhere you go. You must change your consciousness now, before you can see positive results in your life. Then when the new job comes into your life, it will be good, and you will appreciate it and enjoy it.

So, if you hate the job you have, then your affirmation is: I ALWAYS LOVE WHERE I WORK. I HAVE THE BEST JOBS. I AM ALWAYS APPRECIATED. By continually affirming this, you are creating a new personal law for yourself. The Universe will have to respond in kind. Life will always pick the most appropriate channels to bring forth your good, if you allow it.

Do What You Love

If you were raised with the belief that you must "work hard" to earn a living, it is time to let that belief go. Use the affirmation: WORK IS EASY AND FUN FOR ME, or I ENJOY

ALL MY WORK. Keep repeating your affirmation until your consciousness changes. Do what you love and the money will come. Love what you do and the money will come. You have a right to enjoy earning money. Your responsibility to Life is to participate in enjoyable activities. As you find a way to do something that you enjoy, Life will show you the way to prosperity and abundance. Almost always, that activity is playful and joyful. Our inner guidance never gives us "shoulds." The purpose of life is to play. When work becomes play, it is fun and rewarding. Negative attitudes about work create toxins in the body.

If you have been fired, please get over the bitterness as quickly as you can, for bitterness will not bring good into your life. Affirm often: I BLESS MY FORMER BOSS WITH LOVE. OUT OF THIS, ONLY GOOD WILL COME. I AM NOW MOVING INTO MY GREATER GOOD. I AM SAFE AND ALL IS WELL. Then use the affirmation for creating a new job.

It is not what happens to us, but how we handle it. If Life gives you lemons, make lemonade. If the lemons are rotten, then take out the seeds and plant them in order to grow new lemons. Or, you could make compost fertilizer.

Sometimes when we get very close to our dreams, we become so frightened of having what we really want that we begin to sabotage ourselves. As hard as it is to imagine, we are doing this in a mistaken effort to protect ourselves. Making such a big move, having the ideal job, earning really good money, can be a very frightening undertaking. What if I fail? What if people won't like me? What if I am not happy?

These questions represent the part of you that is very afraid of the fulfillment of your dreams. Often, our inner child is the key to our fears. It is time to be very loving, patient, and gentle with yourself. Reassure your inner child, love it, and make it feel safe. A wonderful book that can assist you in accessing inner fears and feelings is Lucia Capaccione's *Recovery of Your Inner Child*. The book uses journaling techniques to promote healing and release. Just remember to say often: I AM SAFE IN THE UNIVERSE, AND ALL LIFE LOVES AND SUPPORTS ME.

Your Thoughts Can Help You Create the Perfect Job

Don't get stuck with the belief that it is hard to get a job. That may be true for many, but it does not have to be true for you. You only need one job. Your clear consciousness will open the pathway for you. Too many people have so much faith in fear. When there is a shift in the economy, the masses immediately buy into all the negative aspects and constantly talk about it and dwell on it. What you dwell on and accept in consciousness becomes true for you.

When you hear of negative trends in business or in the economy, immediately affirm: IT MAY BE TRUE FOR SOME, BUT IT IS NOT TRUE FOR ME. I ALWAYS PROSPER NO MATTER WHERE I AM OR WHAT IS GOING ON. As you think and speak, you are creating your future experiences. Be very careful how you talk about your prosperity. You always have the option of choosing poverty thinking or prosperity thinking. For at least the next week, notice how you talk about money, work, career, the economy, savings, and retirement. Listen to yourself. Make sure the words are not creating poverty now or in the future.

Another thing that can contribute to poverty thinking is dis-honesty, in any form. Many people think that it is normal and natural to take home paper clips and other supplies from the office or wherever they work. They forget or are not aware that whatever you TAKE from Life, Life will TAKE from you. Lifting even small things is saying to Life that you cannot afford to buy these for yourself, and it keeps you stuck in limitation.

When you take from Life, Life always takes more from you. You might take paper clips and lose an important phone call. You could take money and lose a relationship. The last time I knowingly took something (in 1976), it was a postage stamp, and a $300 check that was coming to me in the mail was lost. It was an expensive way to learn a lesson, but well worth it in the long run. So if money is a big issue with you, look to where you might be halting the flow. If you have taken a bunch of stuff from work, take it back. You will never prosper until you do.

Life abundantly supplies all that it requires for sustaining itself. When we recognize this concept and incorporate it into our belief system, then we experience greater prosperity and abundance in our own lives.

Perhaps you are thinking of creating your own business; you like the idea of being your own boss and reaping all the profits. This is great if you have the right temperament. But don't just quit your job and strike out on your own until you have really explored all the side issues. Can you motivate yourself to work if no one is standing over you? Are you willing to put in the 10 to 12 hours a day you may need to work for the first year? New businesses need the dedication of the owner until there are enough profits to hire some help. I worked ten-hour days, seven days a week, for a long time.

I always suggest beginning a new business on a part-time basis. Work on this project after normal working hours and on weekends until you are sure this is what you want to do.

Be sure the business is making enough profit for you to live on before you cut the ties to a regular salary. I began my publishing firm with one book and one tape. I worked in my bedroom with my 90-year-old mother helping me. We would mail out books and tapes at night. It took me two years before there was enough profit to hire an assistant. It was a nice sideline, but it was a long time before Hay House became a real business.

So, when you feel the first inclinations of wanting to go into business on your own, use the affirmation: IF THIS ENTERPRISE IS FOR MY HIGHEST GOOD AND GREATEST JOY, THEN LET IT MOVE FORWARD EASILY AND EFFORTLESSLY. Pay attention to all the signs around you. If delays and obstacles come up, know that this is not the time for you to go ahead. If everything falls into place easily, then go for it, but on a part-time basis to begin with. You can always expand, but it is sometimes hard to retreat.

If you are concerned about bosses, co-workers, customers, the workspace, the building, or any aspect of your new business, remember that you are the one who is making personal laws for yourself about your career. Change your beliefs, and you will change your working life.

Remember: *you* decide what you want your working life to be like. Create positive affirmations to achieve it. Then declare these affirmations often. You CAN have the working life you want!

AFFIRMATIONS FOR IMPROVING YOUR WORK LIFE

I ALWAYS WORK FOR PEOPLE WHO RESPECT ME AND PAY ME WELL.

I ALWAYS HAVE WONDERFUL BOSSES.

I GET ALONG WITH ALL MY CO-WORKERS IN AN ATMOSPHERE OF MUTUAL RESPECT.

EVERYONE AT WORK LOVES ME.

I ALWAYS ATTRACT THE NICEST CUSTOMERS, AND THEY ARE A JOY TO SERVE.

MY WORKSPACE IS A PLEASURE TO BE IN.

I LOVE THE BEAUTY THAT SURROUNDS ME AT WORK.

IT IS A PLEASURE TO COME TO WORK; I LOVE THE NICE, SAFE NEIGHBORHOOD.

IT IS EASY FOR ME TO FIND JOBS.

WORK ALWAYS COMES MY WAY WHEN I WANT IT.

I ALWAYS GIVE 100 PERCENT AT WORK, AND IT IS GREATLY APPRECIATED.

PROMOTIONS COME EASILY TO ME.

MY INCOME IS CONSTANTLY INCREASING.

MY BUSINESS IS EXPANDING BEYOND MY EXPECTATIONS.

I ATTRACT MORE BUSINESS THAN I CAN HANDLE.

THERE IS PLENTY FOR EVERYONE, INCLUDING MYSELF.

MY WORK IS FULFILLING AND SATISFYING.

I AM HAPPY IN MY WORK.

I HAVE A GREAT CAREER.

❀ ❀ ❀

I AM SAFE IN THE BUSINESS WORLD

I know that the thoughts in my mind have everything to do with my working conditions, so I consciously choose my thoughts. My thoughts are supportive and positive. I choose prosperity thinking; therefore, I am prosperous. I choose harmonious thoughts; therefore, I work in a harmonious atmosphere. I love getting up in the morning knowing that I have important work to do today. I have challenging work that is deeply fulfilling. My heart glows with pride when I think of the work that I do. I am ALWAYS employed, always productive. Life is good. And so it is!

❀ ❀ ❀

🌿 Chapter Six 🌿

BODY...MIND...SPIRIT!

---

*"I am progressing on my spiritual path
at the pace that is just right for me."*

Trust Your Inner Wisdom

Deep at the center of our being there is an infinite well of love, an infinite well of joy, an infinite well of peace, and an infinite well of wisdom. This is true for each and every one of us. Yet how often do we get in touch with these treasures within us? Do we do it once a day? Once in a while? Or are we totally unaware that we have these inner treasures?

Just for a moment, close your eyes and connect with that part of yourself. It only takes a breath to go to your center. Go to that infinite well of love within you. Feel the love. Let it grow and expand. Go to that infinite well of joy within you. Feel the joy. Let it grow and expand. Now go to that infinite well of peace within you. Feel that peace. Let it grow and expand. Now go to that infinite well of wisdom within you, that part of you that is totally connected to all the wisdom in the universe—past, present, and future. Trust that wisdom. Let it grow and expand. As you take another breath and come back to your space, keep the knowledge, keep the feeling. Many times today and many, many times tomorrow and each and every day of your life, remind yourself of the treasures that are always within you—and just a breath away.

These treasures are a part of your spiritual connection and are vital to your well-being. Body, mind, and spirit—we need to be balanced on all three levels. A healthy body, a happy mind, and a good, strong spiritual connection are all necessary for our overall balance and harmony.

One of the major benefits of a strong spiritual connection is that we can live wonderful, creative, fulfilling lives. And we will automatically release so many burdens that most people carry.

We will no longer need to be fearful or carry shame and guilt. As we feel our oneness with all of life, we will drop anger and hatred, prejudice, and the need to be judgmental. As we become one with the healing power of the Universe, we will no longer need illness. And, I believe we will be able to reverse the aging process. Burdens are what age us; they drag down our spirits.

We Can Change the World

If each one of us reading this book would practice getting in touch with the treasures within us on a daily basis, we could literally change the world. People living the truth change the world. For the truth of our being is that we are filled with unconditional love. We are filled with incredible joy. We are filled with serene peace. We are connected to infinite wisdom.

What we need to do is to know it and live it! Today we are mentally preparing for tomorrow. The thoughts we think, the words we speak, the beliefs we accept, shape our tomorrows. Every morning, stand in front of a mirror and affirm to yourself: I AM FILLED WITH UNCONDITIONAL LOVE, AND I EXPRESS IT TODAY. I AM FILLED WITH JOY, AND I EXPRESS IT TODAY. I AM FILLED WITH PEACE, AND I SHARE IT TODAY. I AM FILLED WITH INFINITE WISDOM, AND I PRACTICE IT TODAY. AND THIS IS THE TRUTH ABOUT ME. Now that is a powerful way to start your day! You can do it.

Remember, our spiritual connection does not need a middle man such as a church, a guru, or even a religion. We can pray and meditate quite easily by ourselves. Churches and gurus and religions are nice if they are supportive of the individual. Yet, it is important that we know that we all have a direct pipeline to the source of all of life. When we are consciously connected to this source, our life flows in wondrous ways.

So how do we become connected, or re-connected—for we were all well connected when we first came to this world. Perhaps our parents had lost their own connection and taught us that we were alone and lost in life. Perhaps our parents' parents had chosen a religion that gave power to the priesthood and not to the people. There are several religions that tell us: "We are born sinners and lower than the worms of the dust." There are also religions that denigrate women and/or certain classes or groups of people. These are some of the ways we forget who we really are—divine, magnificent expressions of Life.

Yet our souls are always seeking greater growth and integration, an opportunity to heal and express all that we are. Sometimes it is very difficult to understand the methods our souls use to promote our growth. Our personalities, the part of us we assume in order to participate on the Earth plane, have certain expectations and needs. We become afraid, resistant, and sometimes angry when our expectations, such as material advancements, aren't immediately met. It is in these moments, more than any other, that we must hold fast to our faith that there is a higher power working in our lives and that if we are open and willing to grow and change, that things will work out for our highest good.

Often our most painful moments, the times that stretch our personality the furthest, are the moments that provide us with the greatest opportunity for growth. These become an occasion for you to develop greater self-love and greater self-trust. It may or may not comfort you to know that many people are seemingly experiencing setbacks in their lives as well. We are at a place of accelerated growth on this planet. Now more than ever is the time to be extra loving and patient with yourself. Do not resist any opportunity for growth. In times of difficulty, it is important to practice gratitude and blessings as much as you are able.

Pain is always our personality's resistance to new growth. We are all very resistant to change, because we are not very trusting that, ultimately, Life is working perfectly and we are exactly where we need to be, experiencing exactly what we need to in order to grow and evolve into our full potential as a wondrous being in a magnificent universe. We are always in a process of positive growth.

Events in our lives are only experiences. Our experiences are not our identity or our self-worth. We do not want to focus attention on the experience. For instance, we do not want to say: "I am a failure," but rather, "I have had the experience of failure, and I am now in recovery." Growth is just changing the way we look at things.

Life is a learning process. We are here to learn and to grow. Not knowing is not a crime. Not knowing is simply ignorance or lack of understanding. So we don't want to judge ourselves or others for not knowing. Life will always be larger than our ability to grasp it. We are all in a process of learning, growing, and gaining more understanding. Yet, we will never "know it all."

Getting still and going within helps us to find the answers we need for this time in our lives. When we ask for assistance or even call for help, it is our inner self that responds.

Connecting Through Meditation

Getting in touch with the treasures within you is one way of connecting with the source of Life. For within you are all the answers to all the questions you shall ever ask. Wisdom past, present, and future is available to you. The source of Life knows everything. Some people call this connecting process *meditation.*

Meditation is a process that is so simple, and yet there is much confusion about it. Some people are afraid to meditate because they think it is spooky or weird or has something to do with the occult. We often fear that which we do not understand. Still other people lament that they can't meditate because they are always thinking. Well, it is the nature of the mind to think; you will never turn the mind off completely. Continuing to regularly practice meditation will help to quiet the mind. Meditation is a way of bypassing the chatter of the mind to go to the deeper levels, to connect with the inner wisdom.

We are worthy of taking time each day to get in touch with the inner voice, to listen to the answers that come from the inner master. If we don't, then we are only operating on 5 to 10 percent of what is really available to us.

There are many methods of learning to meditate. There are all sorts of classes and books. It could be as simple as sitting in silence with the eyes closed for a short period of time. You might go through the following steps if you're just beginning to meditate:

- You can sit quietly. Close your eyes, take one deep breath, relax your body, and then just concentrate on your breathing. Pay attention to your breathing. Don't try to breathe in a special way. Just be aware of how you are breathing. You will notice that after a few minutes, your breathing will slow down. This is normal and natural as your body relaxes.

- It often helps to count while breathing. One on the inhale, two on the exhale. Three on the inhale, and four on the exhale. Continue in this manner until you reach ten. Then begin again at one. After you do this for a while, you may find your mind wandering to a football game or your shopping list. That's all right. When you notice that you are not counting, just begin again at one, and continue with your counting. The wandering of the mind will happen several times. Each time, gently bring it back to the simple counting routine. That is all there is to it.

This simple form of meditation calms the mind and the body and helps create the connection with our inner wisdom. The benefits of meditation are cumulative. The more often you meditate, the longer you continue to meditate, the better it gets. You will find yourself being more peaceful during the day when you are just going about your ordinary business. And if a crisis comes up, you will handle it in a calmer way.

I often suggest that people begin with just five minutes of sitting or breathing or counting, or whatever form of meditation you choose. Do this once a day for a week or two. Then you might progress to doing it for five minutes twice a day—first thing in the morning and in the early evening. Perhaps you might try meditating right after work, or when you get home at night. The body and the mind love routine. If you can manage to do your meditation at more or less the same time every day, the benefits will increase.

Don't expect much of anything to happen for the first month. Just do your practice. Your mind and body are adjusting to a new rhythm, a new sense of peacefulness. If it is difficult to sit still at the beginning, and if you find that you keep peeking at your watch, use a timer. After a few days, your body will adjust to the time period, and you can discard the timer.

Be gentle with yourself as you learn meditation. No matter what you do, YOU ARE NOT DOING ANYTHING

WRONG. You are learning a new skill. It will get easier and easier. In a relatively short period of time, your body will look forward to the meditation periods.

The ideal time periods to practice meditation are 20 minutes in the morning and 20 minutes in the later afternoon or early evening. Do not be discouraged if it takes you quite some time to work up to this amount of meditation. Just do what you can. Five minutes EVERY DAY is better than twenty minutes once a week.

Many people use a mantra. This can be an Indian Sanskrit word like *om* or *hu,* or a soothing word such as *love* or *peace,* or two words. Instead of counting your breathing, you would use the mantra/word on the inhalation and the exhalation. You may choose two or three words to be your mantra, such as "I am" or "God is," or "I am love" or "All is well." Use one or two words on the inhalation and the other word on the exhalation. Harold Benson, the author of *The Relaxation Response,* has people use the word *one* as they meditate, which also yields excellent results.

So you see, the word or the method is not important. The stillness and the repetition of the gentle breathing are.

A popular form of meditation is TM, or Transcendental Meditation. TM offers a program that gives you a simple mantra to use and some guidance classes. However, these classes have become rather expensive. If you want to spend the money, that's fine; they are a nice bunch of people to be around. But know that you can also achieve great results on your own.

Many community yoga classes begin and end with a short meditation. These classes are usually quite inexpensive, and you can learn a series of gentle stretching exercises that are very beneficial to the body. If you go to your local health food store or community center, I am sure you will find more than one meditation or yoga class listed on their bulletin board.

Religious Science and Unity churches often teach meditation classes. Senior citizen groups and even some hospitals have classes in meditation. If you visit the bookstores or libraries in your area, you will find that there are many books on meditation, some easier to understand than others.

Health programs such as Dr. Dean Ornish's Healthy Heart Program, and Dr. Deepak Chopra's Body, Mind & Spirit Program also include meditation as an important part of the wellness process. (See the Self-Help Resources section in the Appendix for contact information.)

But no matter where or how you learn to meditate, whatever method you begin with, you will in time develop your own form of meditation. Your inner wisdom and intelligence will subtlely alter your process until it is just right for you.

For myself, I began meditating many years ago using a mantra. Because I was still so uptight and frightened at the time, every time I meditated I would get a headache. This lasted for three weeks. As my body and mind began to relax, perhaps for the first time in my life, the headaches ceased. I have been meditating ever since, and I have attended many classes over the years. They each offer a slightly different method of meditation. All methods have benefits, although they may not all be right for you.

Like anything else in life, find the method of meditation that works best for you. You may choose to change methods over the years. And I am sure you will.

Remember, meditation is merely a way of you getting in touch with your own inner guidance. While we are always connected with this guidance as we go about our day, it is easier for us to consciously connect when we sit quietly and listen.

How I Meditate

My personal routines do change from time to time. For today, I always meditate in the morning; it is the best way for me to begin my day. I often meditate in the afternoon, but not always. My morning meditation is usually done sitting in bed. I close my eyes and take a conscious breath or two. Then silently I say, "What is it I need to know?" or "This is the beginning of a good day." Then I allow myself to go into the silence and just be. Sometimes I will notice my breath, and sometimes I won't. Sometimes I notice thoughts, and when I do, I will just observe them. I might acknowledge to myself, "Oh, that's a worry thought, or that's a business thought, or that's a loving thought." I just let the thoughts pass through.

After about 20 or 30 minutes, when I intuitively know that it is time to finish, I take a deep breath. Then I do a form of treatment or prayer, which I say aloud. Perhaps it might go like this:

"There is one infinite power in the Universe, and this power is right where I am. I am not lost or alone or abandoned or helpless. I am one with the Power that created me. If there is any belief within me that would deny this truth, then I erase it right here and now. I know I am a Divine, Magnificent, Expression of Life. I am one with Infinite Wisdom, Love, and Creativity. I am an example of vibrant health and energy. I am loving and loved. I am peaceful. This day is a glorious expression of Life. Each experience I have is joyous and loving. I bless with Divine Love my body, my pets, my home, my work, and each and every person I come into contact with today. This is a great day, and I rejoice in it! And so it is!"

Then I open my eyes, get up, and enjoy my day!

SPIRITUAL AFFIRMATIONS

(Perhaps you haven't learned to feel connected yet. Well, affirmations can help in this area, too. You can say all of the following each day, or just pick one or two to use until you develop some peacefulness and inner knowing within you.)

I HAVE A STRONG SPIRITUAL CONNECTION.

I FEEL AT ONE WITH ALL OF LIFE.

I BELIEVE IN A LOVING GOD.

LIFE SUPPORTS ME AT EVERY TURN.

I TRUST LIFE TO BE THERE FOR ME.

THE POWER THAT CREATED THE WORLD BEATS
    MY HEART.

I AM DIVINELY GUIDED AT ALL TIMES.

I HAVE A SPECIAL GUARDIAN ANGEL.

I AM DIVINELY PROTECTED AT ALL TIMES.

LIFE/GOD LOVES ME.

I AM SAFE WHEREVER I TURN.

🌺 🌺 🌺

Life is my help in every need
Life does my every hunger feed
Life walks beside me
Guides my way
Through every moment of the day.
All things I am, can do, and be
Is because Life loves me.

🌺 🌺 🌺

❦ Chapter Seven ❦

ELDERS OF EXCELLENCE

"How old would you be if you didn't know how old you were?"
— Dr. Wayne W. Dyer

My Beliefs About Aging

For generations, we have allowed the numbers that correspond to how many years we have been on the planet to tell us how to feel and how to behave. As with any other aspect of life, what we mentally accept and believe becomes true for us. Well, it is time to change our beliefs about aging. When I look around and see frail, sick, frightened older people, I say to myself; "It doesn't have to be that way." Many of us have learned that by changing our thinking, we can change our lives. So I know we can make aging a positive, vibrant, healthy experience.

I am now in my 68th year, and I am a big, strong, healthy girl. In many ways, I feel younger than I did at 30 or 40 because I no longer feel the pressures to conform to certain standards imposed by society. I am free to do what I want. I no longer search for anyone's approval, nor do I care what anyone says about me. I please myself much more often. Peer pressure has definitely become less important. In other words, for the first time in my life, I am putting myself first. And it feels good.

There was a time when I allowed the media and so-called authority figures to dictate my behavior, to make judgments about what I wore and which products I bought. Back then, I truly believed that if I did not use all the products that were advertised, then I was not "acceptable." One day, I realized that using all these products only made me acceptable for one day. The next day, I had to start over, I remember spending endless hours plucking my eyebrows in order to be acceptable. That all seems so silly at this point in my life.

Aging with Wisdom

Part of wisdom is knowing what is right for us, sticking to those beliefs, and then releasing all the rest. I do not mean that one need never explore anything new. We want to learn and grow all the time. What I do mean is that it's important to separate the "need" from the "hype" and make your own decisions. Make your own decisions about *everything*, including anything I have told you in this book. While I feel that my ideas have a lot of worth, you have every right to dismiss every one of them. Only use whatever works best for you.

It is unfortunate that from the first moment we are propped up in front of the TV until the last time we turn on the set, we are bombarded with advertisements and inane concepts about life. Little children are targeted as consumers and are expected to beg their parents for certain foods and toys. We are told what to want and what to possess. Few parents teach their children how phony the ads on TV are, how many lies and exaggerations they contain. How could they? These parents were also raised on television ballyhoo.

So, as we grow up, we turn into mindless consumers, buying whatever we are told to buy, doing whatever "they" tell us to do. And believing in all authority figures and whatever we see in print. When we are children, this is understandable, but as adults we need to examine and question everything. If something does not make sense for us, if it is not for our highest good, then it is not right for us. Wisdom is learning when to say no to people, places, things, and experiences that do not benefit us. Wisdom is the ability to examine our belief systems and our relationships to make sure that what we are doing or accepting is for our greatest good.

Why do I buy this product? Why do I work at this job? Why do I have these friends? Why do I choose this religion?

Why do I live here? Why do I believe this about myself? Why do I look at life this way? Why do I feel this way about men/women? Why do I fear or look forward to my later years? Why do I vote the way that I do?

Do your answers make you feel good about yourself and about Life? Do you do things in a certain way only because that is the way you have always done it, or is that the way your parents taught you to do it?

What are you teaching your children about aging? What is the example you are giving them? Do they see a dynamic, loving person, enjoying each day and looking forward to the future? Or are you a bitter, frightened person, dreading your elder years and expecting to be sick and alone? OUR CHILDREN LEARN FROM US! And so do our grandchildren. What kind of elder years do you want to help them envision and create?

Learn to love who you are and where you are, and you will move forward, appreciating each and every moment of your life. This is the example you want to teach your children so that they too can enjoy happy, wonderful lives until the very end.

Learning to Love Your Body

The child who does not feel good about herself or himself will search for reasons to hate his or her body. Because of the intense pressure placed upon us by the advertising world, we often believe that there is something wrong with our bodies. If only we could be thin enough, blond enough, tall enough, if our noses were bigger or smaller, if we had a more dazzling smile—the list goes on and on. So, while we are all young at one point, few of us have ever measured up to the current standards of beauty.

The youth-worshipping cult we have created has added to the discomfort with which we regard our bodies, not to mention our fear of wrinkles. We see every change in our face and body as something to be disdained. What a pity! What a terrible way to feel about ourselves. And yet it is only a thought, and a thought can be changed. The way we choose to perceive our bodies and ourselves is a learned concept. The belief in aging coupled with the feeling of self-hatred so many people have, has caused our life expectancy to be less than 100 years. We are in the process of discovering the thoughts, feelings, attitudes, beliefs, intentions, words, and actions that allow us to live long and healthy lives.

I would like to see everyone loving and treasuring their magnificent selves, inside and out. If you do not feel good about a part of your body, ask yourself why. Where did you get this notion? Did someone tell you that your nose was not straight enough? Who told you that your feet were too big or that your bust was too small? Whose standards are you following? By accepting these concepts, you are injecting anger and hatred into your own body. The sad fact of the matter is that the cells in our bodies cannot do their best work if they are surrounded by hatred.

It's the same as if you went to work every day and your boss hated you. You would never be comfortable, nor could you do a good job. However, if you work in an atmosphere of love and approval, your creativity can blossom in ways that will surprise you. Your cells respond to the way you feel about them. Every thought we think is creating a chemical reaction in our bodies. We can either bathe our cells in a healing atmosphere or we can create poisonous reactions within us. I have noticed that when people get sick, they often direct anger to the affected part of the body. And the result? The healing process is delayed.

So, you can see how crucial it is to our own well-being to constantly love and appreciate the magnificent beings that we are. Our body (our skinsack, as the Chinese say), or the suit that we have chosen to wear in this lifetime, is a wondrous invention. It is just perfect for us. The intelligence within us beats our hearts, gives breath to our body, and knows how to heal a cut or a broken bone. Everything that goes on in our body is miraculous. If we would honor and appreciate every part of our bodies, then our health would greatly improve.

If there is some part of your body that you are not happy with, then take a month and continually put love into that area. Literally tell your body that you love it. You might even apologize for having hated it in the past. This exercise may sound simplistic, but it works. Love yourself inside and out.

The love you create for yourself now will stay with you for the rest of your life. Just as we learned to hate ourselves, so too can we learn to love ourselves. It only takes willingness and a bit of practice.

Feeling vital and energetic is much more important to me than a wrinkle or two or even more. *Cosmopolitan* magazine editor Helen Gurley Brown was on the Larry King show not too long ago, and I heard her say over and over again, "Getting old is the pits! It's the pits! I hate getting old!" I couldn't help thinking, What a terrible affirmation to keep repeating. My suggestion would be to affirm: I LOVE MY ELDER YEARS. THEY ARE THE BEST YEARS OF MY LIFE.

Releasing Sickness and Dis-ease

For a long time, people were unaware that their thoughts and actions had any relation to their health or lack of it. Today, even the medical profession is beginning to acknowledge the body/mind connection. Dr. Deepak Chopra, author of the bestseller *Ageless Body, Timeless Mind,* was invited by Sharp Hospital, a prominent West Coast medical institution, to set up a body/mind clinic there. Dr. Dean Ornish, who practices the holistic treatment of heart dis-ease, has been endorsed by Mutual of Omaha Insurance Company. This huge corporation is now allowing its claimants to receive his treatment under their plan. They have recognized that it is far less expensive to pay for a week's stay at Dr. Ornish's clinic than to pay for open-heart surgery.

This surgery is very expensive, $50,000 to $80,000 per procedure. What many people don't realize is that this surgery only unclogs the arteries for the moment. Bypass surgery is not a long-term solution unless we change our thinking and our diet. We could have done that in the first place and avoided all the pain and suffering and expense. We want to love and take care of our bodies. Drugs and surgery won't do it alone.

In the coming years, I foresee the advent of body/mind clinics at hospitals throughout the country, with insurance companies willingly paying for these treatments. Those who will benefit the most are the people who learn to take care of their own health. They will discover what it means to be truly healthy. I see doctors teaching health practices to their patients instead of just prescribing drugs and surgery for ailments, as they do now. We have many dis-ease care programs, but very few health care programs. We are being taught how to handle dis-ease, rather than how to promote health. I believe that in the near future, alternative, or complementary, medicine, will merge with technological medicine to create true wellness programs for all of us.

I see health as preventive medicine and care, not just crisis and sickness care. A good health care plan would include education. It would teach us all how to contribute to our wellness. Everyone could learn the principles of the mind/body connection, the value of nutrition and exercise, and the use of herbs and vitamins. We could all explore other complementary natural ways of creating wellness among our population.

USA Today reported in 1993 that 34 percent of the U.S. population, or 80 million people, use some form of alternative health care, including chiropractic treatment. They reported that Americans have made over 250 million office visits to alternative health care practitioners. Many of these visits resulted from the fact that the medical profession could no longer meet their needs. I think the number would be much greater if the insurance companies would pay for these visits.

We have set up a system where mutilation and poison is the accepted way of treating illness, and the natural ways of healing are considered un-natural. One day all the insurance companies will discover that it is much cheaper for them to pay for an acupuncture or nutritional treatment than for a visit to the hospital, and it will often yield better results.

It is time for all of us to take our power back from the medical and pharmaceutical industries. We have been buffeted about by high-tech medicine, which is very expensive and which often destroys our health. It is time for all of us, and especially the elders who have less time, to learn to take control of our own bodies and create good health, thereby saving millions of lives and billions of dollars.

Are you aware that 50 percent of all bankruptcies are caused by hospital bills, and that the average person who enters the hospital with a fatal illness will lose all of their life savings during the last ten days that they are there? We definitely need to make some changes in the way our health care is now being handled!

We CAN Control Our Own Bodies

Getting old and sick used to be the norm for most people in our society. But it no longer has to be that way. We are at a point where we can take control of our own bodies. As we learn more about nutrition, we will come to the realization that what we put into our bodies has a great deal to do with how we feel and look and whether we are healthy or not. We will be more apt to reject manufacturers' advertising claims if we find that they are not valid.

A whole program of health-care education could be launched and supported by elders. If we could get organizations such as the American Association of Retired Persons (AARP)—with their 30 million members—to really support health care rather than illness care, we could make enormous positive changes. However, we cannot wait for them to get on the bandwagon. We need to learn everything we can about how to handle our own health care now.

Until we can really teach the people that they are greatly responsible for their health and their dis-ease, there will be no point in living longer. I would like to help all people move into their later years vibrantly healthy.

Fear Is So Limiting

I see so much fear among elderly people—fear of change, poverty, illness, senility, loneliness, and most of all, fear of death. I truly believe that all this fear is unnecessary. It is something we have been taught. It has been programmed into us. It is just a habitual thinking pattern, and it can be changed. Negative thinking is prevalent among so many people in their later years and, as a result, they live out their lives in discontent.

It is crucial that we always keep in mind that what we think and say becomes our experiences. As such, we will pay attention to our thoughts and speaking patterns so that we may shape our lives in accordance with our dreams. We may say wistfully, "Oh, I wish I could have or would have or that I could be or would be...," but we don't seem to use the words and thoughts that can actually make those wishes a reality. Instead, we think every negative thought we know and then wonder why our lives are not working in the way that we would like. As I mentioned earlier, we all think about 60,000 thoughts a day, and MOST of them are the same thoughts we thought yesterday and the day before that! To counteract this thinking rut, every morning I say to myself, " I HAVE A NEW UNDERSTANDING OF LIFE. I NOW THINK THOUGHTS I HAVE NEVER THOUGHT BEFORE, NEW CREATIVE THOUGHTS."

Consequently, if you have fearful thoughts about change, you could say: I AM AT PEACE WITH THE EVER-CHANGING PATTERNS OF LIFE, AND I AM ALWAYS SAFE. If you fear poverty, try: I AM ONE WITH THE UNIVERSAL POWER OF ABUNDANCE, AND I AM ALWAYS PROVIDED FOR BEYOND MY NEEDS. For fear of illness, you might affirm: I AM THE EMBODIMENT OF HEALTH AND

VITALITY, AND I REJOICE IN MY WELLNESS. If you fear getting senile, say: I AM ONE WITH UNIVERSAL WISDOM AND KNOWLEDGE, AND MY MIND IS ALWAYS SHARP AND CLEAR. For loneliness: I AM ONE WITH EACH AND EVERY PERSON ON THIS PLANET, AND I GIVE AND RECEIVE LOVE CONSTANTLY. If you fear spending the last days of your life in a nursing home, state: I ALWAYS LIVE IN MY OWN HOME, HAPPILY TAKING CARE OF MYSELF. For fear of death: I WELCOME EACH STAGE OF MY LIFE, KNOWING THAT LEAVING THE PLANET IS LIKE OPENING A DOOR TO LOVE AND A GLORIOUS NEXT EXPERIENCE.

These statements are all ways of retraining your mind for a more joyous later life. If you affirm these statements whenever fearful thoughts arise, then in time, these thoughts will become true for you. As they become your new truths, you will find that not only will your life change for the better, but your vision of the future will also change. It is a continual process of growth and transformation.

Another wonderful affirmation is: I AM INDEPEN-DENTLY HEALTHY AND WEALTHY.

Finding and Using the Treasures Within

I want to help you create a conscious ideal of your later years, to help you realize that these can be the most rewarding years of your life. Know that your future is always bright, no matter what your age. See your later years becoming your treasure years. You can become an ELDER OF EXCELLENCE.

Many of you are now moving into the ranks of the elders, and it is time to view life in a different way. You don't have to live your later years the way that your parents did. You and I can create a new way of living. We can change all the rules. When we move forward into our future, knowing and using the treasures within, then only good lies before us. We can know and affirm that everything that happens to us is for our highest good and greatest joy, truly believing that we can't go wrong.

Instead of just getting old and giving up and dying, let's make a huge contribution to life. We have the time, we have the knowledge, and we have the wisdom to move out into the world with love and power. Society is facing many challenges at this time. There are many issues and problems of a global nature that require our attention.

We want to reframe how we see the different stages of our life. Interestingly enough, there was a study done at a major university recently on middle age. The researchers discovered that at whatever age you believe is middle age, it is at that time that your body will begin the aging process. You see, the body accepts what the mind decides upon. So, instead of accepting 45 or 50 as middle age, we could easily decide that 75 is the new middle age. The body will willingly accept that, too.

It is aging and life shortening to say, "I don't have enough time." Instead we want to say, "I HAVE MORE THAN ENOUGH TIME, SPACE, AND ENERGY FOR WHAT IS IMPORTANT."

Our life spans have been lengthening since we were first created as a species. We used to live very short lives—first only till our mid-teens, then our twenties, then thirties, then forties. Even at the turn of this century it was considered old to be 50. In 1900 our life expectancy was 47 years. Now we are accepting 80 as a normal life span. Why can't we take a quantum leap in consciousness and make the new level of acceptance 120 or 150 years?!

Yes, of course we need to create the health, wealth, love, compassion, and acceptance to go with this new span of life. When I talk about living to 120, most people exclaim, "Oh, no! I don't want to be sick or poor for all those years." Why do our minds immediately go to limitation thinking? We do not have to equate age with poverty, sickness, loneliness, and death. If that is what we often see around us now, it is because that is what we have created from our past belief systems.

We can always change our belief systems. We once believed the world was flat. Now that is no longer a truth for us. I know we can change what we think and accept as normal. We can live long lives that are healthy, loving, wealthy, wise, and joyous.

Yes, we will need to change our current beliefs. We will need to change the ways we structure our society, our retirement issues, our insurance, our health care. But it *can* be done.

I want to give you hope and inspire you to learn to heal yourselves, which will then allow us to heal society. It is time to restore elders to the top of the heap. As elders, we deserve esteem and honor. But first, we must develop self-esteem and self-worth. It is not something we have to earn. It is something we develop in our own consciousness.

Turning Your Life Around

You have the power to alter your life so that you will not even recognize your old self. You can go from illness to health, from loneliness to love. You can go from poverty to security and fulfillment. You can go from guilt and shame to self-confidence and self-love. You can go from a feeling of worthlessness to feeling creative and powerful. You CAN make your later years a wonderful time!

113

It is time for all of us to be all that we can be during our elder years. This is the future that I look forward to. Join me. Let's begin a movement called Elders of Excellence so that as we move into our Treasure Years, we contribute more to society, rather than less.

When I first began my healing work, I concentrated on teaching people to love themselves, to drop resentment, to forgive, to release old, limiting beliefs and patterns. This was wonderful, and as so many of you have attested to, you were able to improve the quality of your lives to a remarkable degree. This individual work is still extremely helpful and needs to continue until every person on this planet is living a life full of health, happiness, contentment, fulfillment, and love.

Now is the time for us to take these ideas and apply them to society as a whole. To bring them into the mainstream. To help improve the quality of life for everyone. Our reward will be a peaceful, loving world where we, as elders, can leave our doors unlocked, walk around freely at night, and know that our neighbors are here to accept us, support us, and help us if necessary.

We can change our belief systems. But in order to do so, we, as Elders of Excellence, need to get out of the victim mentality. As long as we see ourselves as being hapless, powerless individuals, as long as we depend on the government to "fix" things for us, we will never progress as a group. However, when we band together and come up with creative solutions for our later years, then we have real power, and we can change our nation and our world for the better.

A Few Words for the Baby Boomers

I'd like to say a few words to you baby boomers out there who are now just beginning to enter your fifties.

How do you want to mature? How do you want America to mature? What we create for ourselves, we create for our country. We will have more people living long lives in the next few decades than ever before in history. Do we want to continue with the same-old, same-old? Or are we ready to take a quantum leap in consciousness and create a totally new way of living for those in their later years?

We simply cannot wait for the government to change everything for us. Washington, D.C., has become a hotbed of special interests and greed. We need to look within, instead, and find our own treasures, our own wisdom, and then dispense it with love to all the rest of society.

Baby boomers, pre-baby boomers, and post-baby boomers: I call upon all of you to join me in moving from the "me" generation to the "we" generation. It's funny—there is a group called the Young Presidents' Organization (the YPOs) who represent youthful leaders in business and society. But most of them are overworked and are killing themselves because they do not take the time to go inside and get in touch with their inner wisdom. They have made their pile of money and now wonder, "Is this all there is?" What they need to do to go from "me" to "we" is to turn themselves on to service to their community and to their country. Why? Because they are the ideal group to be leaders for Elders of Excellence!

Each of us, including our current politicians, needs to take the time every day to sit in silence. If we don't take the time to go within and connect with our inner wisdom, we won't know the best decisions to make. It is almost an act of arrogance to assume responsibility for others and not take the time to go within and get in touch with the universal guidance.

I foresee a world where Leaders of Excellence and Elders of Excellence can work together hand in hand to heal America. The Leaders of Excellence could easily have fathers and mothers that could be Elders of Excellence. We could all work together to discuss and implement plans to help our society function more productively. And this plan could work in business as well as in many other areas—health care, the arts, whatever your area of work/service. There is room to help out no matter what age you are!

Taking Back Our Power

I so strongly feel that our elders have been treated like a throwaway society, when actually, our elders are the perfect guides to help rebuild our world. There was a time when elders were held in great esteem for their contributions and knowledge, but we have diminished their importance through our creation and worship of a youthful society. What a mistake. Youth is a wonderful thing, but the youths also grow into elders. We all need to look forward to comfortable, peaceful later years.

In astrological terms, a person hasn't even completed one's first Saturn return until the age of 29. Saturn, the teacher, takes 29 years to complete one cycle of an astrological chart. Only after you have had experiences in all 12 areas of your life can you then apply that learning to your current life.

As elders, we need to learn to play again, to have fun, to laugh, to be children if we want. We do not deserve to be thrown into a corner so we can wither and die. And we won't be treated that way unless we allow it. The elders must come back and participate fully in life and share what they know with the younger generation. People often say, "Oh, if only I could do it all over…" Well, you can! By stepping out and taking a leadership role, by once again becoming a complete member of society, you can contribute to a new and better world.

If you or a relative frequent a senior center, instead of talking about your dis-eases, talk about how you can band together and improve your corner of society. What can you do to make life better for everyone? No matter how small your contribution, it has meaning. If all elders contribute something, we can improve our country.

By activating ourselves in all segments of society, we will see our wisdom trickling down to all levels, thereby transforming our country into a place of loving kindness. So, I urge you: Step forward, use your voice, get out in the world, and LIVE! This is an opportunity for you to regain your power and create a legacy that you will be proud to pass on to your grandchildren and to their grandchildren.

It is my fervent desire to inspire and empower elders everywhere to contribute to our country's healing. Elders, you are the generation to turn things around. You are the people. You are the government. You are the ones who can make the changes. And your time is NOW.

We must all stop following leaders who send us down the wrong paths. We must stop believing that greed and selfishness will bring any permanent good into our lives. We must love ourselves first of all and have compassion for ourselves. Then we can share that love and compassion with everyone on the planet. This is OUR world, and we have the ability to turn it into a paradise.

Planetary or global healing is a response to the awareness that what we experience in our outer world is a mirror for the energy patterns within us. An important part of any healing process is to acknowledge our connection and contribution to the whole of Life and to begin the process of projecting positive healing energy out into the world. This is a place where so many of us get stuck in our own energy, unaware of the healing power of giving and sharing. Healing is a continual process, so if we wait until we are "healed" to begin sharing love, we may never have the opportunity to do so.

My Hope for Our Country

I don't have all the answers, but I urge you, those with the knowledge and means to do so, please step forward and help heal this planet of ours.

Our burdens tend to age us. But if each one of us does just a little bit, we can effect profound change. For example, there is a dentist in Los Angeles who began donating free services to the homeless. Can you imagine being homeless and having a root canal act up? This man has said, "If every dentist in Los Angeles would give one free hour a week, all the homeless in the city could be taken care of."

We often feel overwhelmed by our problems, but if we each gave but a fraction of our time to address the issues that affect us, many problems could be solved. Many elders are at an age when they have nothing to lose. They do not have jobs or homes to lose because they have achieved their financial security. Elders who *have* can help elders who *do not* have. I am sure that many of the wealthy elders in this country could be persuaded to part with some of their money if we showed them a way to be honored and admired by society.

It's true that many of our current problems were created by these wealthy elders of my generation who were once on the forefront of corporate greed. They have seen the consequences of selfish, money-grubbing behavior on the part of big business and certain individuals. But now, there is a larger role for these people to play. A part in the healing of America. They can still be the bigwigs, but now they can do so as healers rather than abusers. They can easily donate a few million here and there to make our society great again.

I truly believe that as everyone takes a part in our country's healing process, we can grow younger instead of older. We can "youthen." I know it is possible. It may take until the third generation to attain "youthening" and have it be a normal and natural thing, but today's elders can be the pioneers and lead the way. Some books are now being written on the youthening process. *New Cells, New Bodies, New Lives,* by Virginia Essene, gives us new ideas to think about. I know youthening can be done; it is just a matter of finding out how.

The baby boomers who are approaching their fifties right now can think about how they would like to approach their later years and how they want to give service. The younger generations can change the way they look at the elders and make decisions about how they want to be when they get to that stage.

Children at school are always asked, "What do you want to do when you grow up?" They are taught to plan for their future. We need to take the same attitude and plan for our later years. What do we want to be when we grow older? I want to be an Elder of Excellence, contributing to society in every way I can. Maggie Kuhn, head of the activist group, the Gray Panthers, recently said, "I want to die in an airport, briefcase in hand, just finishing a job well done."

Think about these questions: How can you serve? What will you do to help heal America? What legacy do you want to leave to your grandchildren? These are important questions for us to ask ourselves as we move through our twenties and thirties and forties. Then we will enter our fifties and sixties and still have a world of opportunity before us. I remember hearing someone say recently, "I knew I was getting old when people stopped telling me I had my whole life ahead of me."

Well, you *do* have your "whole life" ahead of you. What else are you going to prepare for—your "whole death"? Of course not! Now is the time to live it up, to acknowledge your self-worth, to take pride in the title, Elders of Excellence.

I honor all of us who have the courage to move forward with the ideas I've presented here. Yes, there might be resistance, there might be some degree of hardship. But so what! We are Elders, and we are invincible!

AFFIRMATIONS FOR ELDERS OF EXCELLENCE

(You might wish to repeat the following affirmations when you wake up in the morning and before you go to sleep at night.)

I AM YOUNG AND BEAUTIFUL...AT EVERY AGE.

I CONTRIBUTE TO SOCIETY IN FULFILLING AND PRODUCTIVE WAYS.

I AM IN CHARGE OF MY FINANCES, MY HEALTH, AND MY FUTURE.

I AM RESPECTED BY ALL WHOM I COME IN CONTACT WITH.

I HONOR AND RESPECT THE CHILDREN AND ADOLESCENTS IN MY LIFE.

I HONOR AND RESPECT ALL THE ELDERS IN MY LIFE.

I LIVE EVERY DAY TO THE FULLEST.

I THINK NEW AND DIFFERENT THOUGHTS EACH DAY.

MY LIFE IS A GLORIOUS ADVENTURE.

I AM OPEN TO EXPERIENCING ALL THAT LIFE HAS TO OFFER.

MY FAMILY IS SUPPORTIVE OF ME, AND I AM SUPPORTIVE OF THEM.

I HAVE NO LIMITATIONS.

I HAVE MY WHOLE LIFE AHEAD OF ME.

I SPEAK UP; MY VOICE IS HEARD BY THE LEADERS IN SOCIETY.

I TAKE THE TIME TO PLAY WITH MY INNER CHILD.

I MEDITATE, TAKE QUIET WALKS, ENJOY NATURE; I ENJOY SPENDING TIME ALONE.

LAUGHTER IS A BIG PART OF MY LIFE; I HOLD NOTHING BACK.

I THINK OF WAYS TO HELP HEAL THE PLANET, AND I IMPLEMENT THEM.

I HAVE ALL THE TIME IN THE WORLD.

🌺   🌺   🌺

MY LATER YEARS ARE
MY TREASURE YEARS

I rejoice in each passing year. My wealth of knowledge grows, and I am in touch with my wisdom. I feel the guidance of angels every step of the way. My later years are my treasure years. I know how to live. I know how to keep myself youthful and healthy. My body is re-newed at every moment. I am vital, vivacious, healthy, fully alive, and contributing to my last day. I am at peace with my age. I create the kind of relationships I want to have. I create the prosperity I need. I know how to be triumphant. My later years are my TREASURE YEARS, and I become an ELDER OF EXCELLENCE. I now contribute to life in every way I can, knowing I am love, joy, peace, and infinite wisdom now and forevermore. And so it is!

🌺   🌺   🌺

🌿 Chapter Eight 🌿

DEATH AND DYING:
OUR SOUL'S TRANSITION

---

*"We come to this planet to learn
certain lessons, and then we move on..."*

Death—A Natural Part of Life

Since I began my work with People with Aids, I have personally known hundreds of people who have died. Being close to some of these people during the end of their lives has given me an understanding of death that I did not have before. I once thought of death as a frightening experience. Now I know it is just a normal, natural part of life. I like to think of death as "leaving the planet."

I believe we each come to this planet to learn certain lessons. When those lessons have been learned, we leave. A lesson for a certain lifetime may be a short one. Perhaps we needed to experience abortion, so we do not make it out of the womb alive. Perhaps there was a soul decision between us and our parents to learn the lessons of love and compassion through infant death. We may have needed only a few days or months and leave by crib death.

Some people use dis-ease as their way to leave the planet. They create a life that does not seem possible to straighten out, so they decide that they would rather leave now and work it out another time. Some people choose to leave the planet in a dramatic fashion—perhaps via a car accident or a plane wreck.

We know that someone has been healed of virtually every dis-ease we have been able to create. And yet many people use dis-ease as a way to leave when it is their time to go. Dying by dis-ease is a socially acceptable way to go.

Whatever way we leave and whenever we leave, I believe it is a soul choice and that it occurs in the perfect time/space sequence. Our soul allows us to leave in the way that is best for us this time around. When we see the larger picture of life, it is impossible for us to judge any one method of leaving.

Overcoming the Fear of Death

I have noticed that the people with the most anger, resentment, and bitterness seem to have the most difficult deaths. There is often struggle, fear, and guilt associated with their passing. Those who have made peace with themselves and understand the value of forgiveness for themselves and others have the most peaceful passings. Those who were taught "Brimstone and Hellfire," on the other hand, are most terrified by the prospect of leaving.

If you fear leaving the planet, I recommend that you read one of the many books that deal with people's near-death experiences. Dr. Raymond Moody's *Life After Life,* and Dannion Bradley's *Saved by the Light* are enlightening and inspirational works that reveal how a close encounter with death can completely alter one's perception of life and also remove all fear of dying.

So just as it is important to know what we believe about different issues in life, it is also most important to be very clear about what we are choosing to believe about death. Many religions, while trying to manipulate us into behaving according to their rules, give us terrifying images of death and life after death. I really do believe it is very wicked to tell anyone that they will burn in hell forever. That sort of talk is pure manipulation. Don't listen to people who sell fear.

So, once again, I suggest that you make a list entitled: "What I Believe About Death." List all the things that come up in your mind. No matter how foolish they sound, they are in your subconscious. If you have a lot of negative messages within you, then do the work to change those beliefs. Meditate, study, read books, and learn to create for yourself a positive, supportive belief in the afterlife.

What we believe becomes true for us. If you believe in hell, then you will probably go there for a while until you awaken to the truth and change your consciousness. I really believe that heaven and hell are states of mind, and we can experience both while here on earth.

Fearing death interferes with living. It is not until we can be at peace with dying that we can really begin living.

A Time to Live and a Time to Die

There comes a time in each person's life when he or she must accept that death is NOW. I believe that we need to be peaceful with the timing, whenever it is. We want to learn to accept death, to allow ourselves to go through the experience it offers with wonder and peace instead of fear.

People usually have very strong views about suicide, and I have been criticized about mine. I think that to kill yourself because a love affair has ended, or because you've gone bankrupt, or because of some other problem of life, is very foolish. We miss the opportunity to learn and to grow. And if we refuse the lesson this time, then in the next life the lesson will surface again.

Remember the many times you have been in trouble and you did not know how you would get out of it? Well, you did, and you are here. You found a solution. What if you had killed yourself over it? Look at all the great living you would have missed.

On the other hand, in some people's lives, there comes a time of great, unyielding physical pain that cannot be alleviated. They are so deeply immersed in an excruciating illness that they have passed the point of no return. I have seen this happen many times with the dis-ease called aids. Who am I to judge anyone in those circumstances who has chosen to take their life? I believe that the so-called Doctor of Death, Dr. Jack Kervorkian, is a very compassionate man who helps terminally ill people end their lives with dignity.

I wrote the following for a dear friend who was consciously dying. It gave him great comfort at the time. Many times during the day and night he would "position himself for maximum peace." I have also used these words for many others who were in the process of leaving....

WE ARE ALWAYS SAFE

We are always safe.
It's only change.
From the moment we are born
We are preparing to be Embraced by the Light
Once more.
Position yourself for Maximum Peace.
Angels surround you
And are guiding you each step of the way.
Whatever you choose
Will be perfect for you.
Everything will happen in
The perfect time-space sequence.
This is a time for Joy
And for Rejoicing.
You are on your way Home
As we all are.

* * *

I have often thought of my own passing as
THE END OF THE PLAY.
The final curtain descends.
The applause is over.
I go to my dressing room and remove my makeup.
The costume is left on the floor.
The character is no longer me.
Naked, I walk to the stage door.
As I open the door, I am met by a smiling face.
It is the new Director,
New script and costume in hand.
I am overjoyed to see all my loyal fans and loved ones waiting.
The applause is loving and deafening.
I am greeted with more love than I have
ever experienced before.
My new role promises to be the most exciting ever.

I know
Life is always good.
Wherever I am
All is well.
I am safe.
See you later.
Bye.

* * *

I ALSO SEE LIFE AS A MOVIE

In each lifetime
We always come into the middle of the movie
And we always leave in the middle of the movie.
There is no right time,
There is no wrong time.
It is only our time.
The soul makes the choice long before we come in.
We have come to experience certain lessons.
We have come to love ourselves.
No matter what "they" did or said
We have come to cherish
Ourselves and others.

When we learn the lesson of love
We may leave with joy.
There is no need for pain or suffering.
We know that next time
Wherever we choose to incarnate
On whatever plane of action
We will take all of the love with us.

* * *

THE TUNNEL OF LOVE

Our Final Exit is one of
Release, Love, and Peace.
We release and let go into the exit tunnel.
At the end of the tunnel, we find
Only Love.
Love such as we have never experienced before.
Total, all-encompassing, unconditional Love
And deep inner Peace.
All the Ones we have ever loved are there,
Waiting and welcoming,
Caring and guiding.
We are never alone again.

It is a time of great rejoicing.
A time of reviewing
Our last incarnation
Lovingly and only to gain Wisdom.

TEARS ARE GOOD, TOO!
Tears are the river of Life.
They carry us through
Experiences that are deeply emotional.

HAPPY ASCENSION!
You know I will join you
In what will seem
Like a twinkling of an eye.

***

One of the last things my friend said to me was, "Are we saying goodbye now?" And I replied, "For this lifetime, yes."

These are some of my ideas on death and dying. Now formulate your own. Just make sure they are comforting and loving.

❧   ❧   ❧

THE LIFE ESSENCE
IS ALWAYS WITH US

I release the past with ease, and I trust the process of Life. I close the door on old hurts, and I forgive everyone, myself included. I visualize a stream in front of me. I take all those old experiences, the old hurts and pains, and I put them all into the stream and watch them begin to dissolve and drift downstream until they totally dissipate and disappear. I am free and everyone in my past is free. I am ready to move forward into the new adventures that await me. Lifetimes come and go, but I am always eternal. I am alive and vital, no matter which plane of action I am on. Love surrounds me, now and forevermore. And so it is!

LOVE YOURSELF AND LOVE YOUR LIFE!

❧   ❧   ❧

101
Power Thoughts
for LIFE!

The thoughts we think and the words we speak are constantly shaping our world and our experiences. Many of us are in an old habit of negative thinking and do not realize the damage we have inflicted upon ourselves. However, we are never stuck, because we can always change our thinking. As we learn to consistently choose positive thoughts, the old, negative ones dissolve away.

So, as you read the following power thoughts, let the affirmations and ideas wash over your consciousness. Your subconscious mind will pick up the ones that are important to you at the moment. These concepts are like fertilizing the soil of your mind. As you absorb them by repetition, you are slowly enriching the very basis of your garden of life. Anything you plant will grow abundantly. I see you vibrant and healthy, surrounded by exquisite beauty, living a life of love and prosperity, filled with joy and laughter. You are on a wonderful pathway of change and growth. Enjoy your trip.

1 MY HEALING IS ALREADY IN PROCESS

Your body knows how to heal itself. Get the negative garbage out of the way. Then love your body. Feed it nourishing foods and beverages. Pamper it. Respect it. Create an atmosphere of wellness. Allow yourself to heal.

My willingness to forgive begins my healing process. I allow the love from my own heart to wash through me, cleansing and healing every part of my body. I know I am worth healing.

2 I TRUST MY INNER WISDOM

There is a place within each of us that is totally connected with the infinite wisdom of the universe. In this place lie all the answers to all the questions we will ever ask. Learn to trust your inner self.

As I go about my daily affairs, I listen to my own guidance. My intuition is always on my side. I trust it to be there at all times. I am safe.

3 I AM WILLING TO FORGIVE

If we sit in a prison of self-righteous resentment, we cannot be free. Even if we don't know exactly how to forgive, we can be willing to forgive. The Universe will respond to our willingness and help us find the way.

Forgiveness of myself and of others releases me from the past. Forgiveness is the answer to almost every problem. Forgiveness is a gift to myself. I forgive, and I set myself free.

4   *I AM DEEPLY FULFILLED BY ALL THAT I DO*

We will never have the opportunity to live this day again, so we want to savor every moment. There is richness and fullness in everything we do.

Each moment of the day is special to me as I follow my higher instincts and listen to my heart. I am at peace in my world and affairs.

5   *I TRUST THE PROCESS OF LIFE*

We are learning how Life works. It is like learning your computer. When you first get a computer, you learn the simple, basic processes—how to turn it on and off, how to open and save a document, how to print. And on that level, your computer works wonders for you. And yet, there is so much more that it can do for you when you learn more of its ways. It is the same thing with Life. The more we learn how it works, the more wonders it performs for us.

There is a rhythm and flow to Life, and I am part of it. Life supports me and brings me only good and positive experiences. I trust the process of Life to bring me my highest good.

6   *I HAVE THE PERFECT LIVING SPACE*

Our living space is always an outpicturing of our current state of consciousness. If we hate where we live now, then no matter where we move, we will end up hating that, too. Bless your current abode with love. Thank it for providing for your needs. Say that you are moving on and that wonderful new people are moving in to take your place. Leave love when you move, and you will feel love in the new place. Before I found my current home, I decided that I wanted to buy a house from people who were in love. Of course, that is exactly what I found. My home is filled with the vibration of love.

I see myself living in a wonderful place. It fulfills all my needs and desires. It's in a beautiful location and is at a price I can easily afford.

7   I CAN RELEASE THE PAST AND FORGIVE EVERYONE

We may not want to let go of old hurts, but holding on to them keeps us STUCK. When I let go of the past, my present moment becomes richer and fuller.

I free myself and everyone in my Life from old past hurts. They are free and I am free to move into new, glorious experiences.

8   THE POINT OF POWER IS ALWAYS IN THE PRESENT MOMENT

No matter how long you have had a problem, you can begin to change in this moment. For as you change your thinking, your Life also changes.

The past is over and done and has no power over me. I can begin to be free in this moment. Today's thoughts create my future. I am in charge. I now take my own power back. I am safe and I am free.

9   I AM SAFE, IT'S ONLY CHANGE

What we believe comes true for us. The more we trust Life, the more Life is there for us.

I cross all bridges with joy and with ease. The "old" unfolds into wonderful new experiences. My Life gets better all the time.

10   *I AM WILLING TO CHANGE*

We all want Life to change and other people to change. But nothing in our world will change until we are willing to make changes in ourselves. We often cling so tightly to habits and beliefs that no longer serve us in a positive way.

I am willing to release old, negative beliefs. They are only thoughts that stand in my way. My new thoughts are positive and fulfilling.

11   *IT'S ONLY A THOUGHT AND A THOUGHT CAN BE CHANGED*

The most frightening scenarios we can conceive of are only thoughts. We can easily refuse to scare ourselves in this way. You want your thoughts to be your best friends—thoughts that shape your world in a positive way. Comforting thoughts, loving thoughts, friendly thoughts, laughing thoughts. Thoughts of wisdom and upliftment.

I am not limited by any past thinking. I choose my thoughts with care. I constantly have new insights and new ways of looking at my world. I am willing to change and to grow.

12   *EVERY THOUGHT I THINK IS CREATING MY FUTURE*

I am constantly aware of my thoughts. I am like a shepherd with a flock of sheep, and if one goes astray, I lovingly herd it back in line. If I notice an unloving, unkind thought going astray, I quickly and consciously replace it with a kind and loving one. The Universe is always listening and responding to my thinking process. I keep the line as clean and clear as I can.

The Universe totally supports every thought I choose to think and to believe. I have unlimited choices about what I can think. I choose balance, harmony, and peace; and I express it in my Life.

13   THERE IS NO BLAME

If we walk a mile in someone else's shoes, then we understand why they behave the way that they do. We were all born beautiful little babies, totally open and trusting of Life, with lots of self-worth and self-esteem. If we are not that way now, then somewhere along the line, someone taught us otherwise. We can unlearn the negativity.

I release the need to blame anyone, including myself. We are all doing the best we can with the understanding, knowledge, and awareness we have.

14   I LET GO OF ALL EXPECTATIONS

If we don't have specific expectations, then we cannot be disappointed. But if we love ourselves and know that only good lies before us, then it doesn't matter what comes up because it will be fulfilling.

I flow freely and lovingly with Life. I love myself. I know that only good awaits me at every turn.

15 *I SEE CLEARLY*

The unwillingness to "see" certain aspects of our lives can cloud our vision. This unwillingness to see is often a form of protection. Optometrists do little to cure eye problems. They only prescribe stronger and stronger glasses. Poor nutrition can also contribute to poor eyesight.

I release all things from my past that cloud my vision. I see the perfection in all of Life. I willingly forgive. I breathe love into my vision, and I see with compassion and understanding. My clear insight is reflected in my outer sight.

16 *I AM SAFE IN THE UNIVERSE AND ALL LIFE LOVES AND SUPPORTS ME*

I carry this affirmation in my wallet. Whenever I reach for money, I see: I AM SAFE IN THE UNIVERSE AND ALL LIFE LOVES AND SUPPORTS ME. It is a good reminder of what is really important in my Life.

I breathe in the fullness and richness of Life. I observe with joy as Life abundantly supports me and supplies me with more good than I can imagine.

17 *MY LIFE IS A MIRROR*

Every person in my Life is a reflection of some part of me. The people I love reflect the loving aspects of myself. The people I dislike reflect those parts of myself that need healing. Every experience in Life is an opportunity for growth and healing.

The people in my Life are really mirrors of me. This affords me the opportunity to grow and to change.

18   I BALANCE MY MASCULINE AND FEMININE SIDES

We all contain masculine and feminine aspects. When these two sides are in balance, then we are whole and complete. The totally macho man is not in touch with the intuitive side of himself. And a weak, wispy feminine woman is not expressing the strong, intelligent side of herself. We all need both sides.

The masculine and feminine parts of me are in perfect balance and harmony. I am at peace and all is well.

19   FREEDOM IS MY DIVINE RIGHT

We are put on this planet with total freedom of choice. And we make these choices in our minds. No person, place, or thing can think for us if we do not allow it. We are the only person who thinks in our mind. In our minds we have total freedom. What we choose to think and believe can change our current circumstances beyond recognition.

I am free to think wonderful thoughts. I move beyond past limitations into freedom. I am now becoming all that I am created to be.

20   I RELEASE ALL FEARS AND DOUBTS

Fears and doubts are only delay mechanisms that keep us from having the good we say we want in our lives. So let them go.

I now choose to free myself from all destructive fears and doubts. I accept myself and create peace in my mind and heart. I am loved and I am safe.

21   DIVINE WISDOM GUIDES ME

Too many of us are unaware that we have within us an inner wisdom that is always on our side. We don't pay attention to our intuition, and then we wonder why Life does not work well. Learn to listen to your inner voice. You do know exactly what to do.

I am guided throughout this day in making right choices. Divine Intelligence continuously guides me in the realization of my goals. I am safe.

22   I LOVE LIFE

Every morning when I wake up, I get to experience another great day—a day I have never lived before. It will have its own special experiences. I am glad to be alive.

It is my birthright to live fully and freely. I give to Life exactly what I want Life to give to me. I am glad to be alive. I love Life!

23   I LOVE MY BODY

I am so delighted to live in my wonderful body. It has been given to me to use for the rest of my Life, and I cherish it and take loving care of it. My body is precious to me. I love every inch of it, inside and out, that which I see and that which I don't see, every organ and gland, every muscle and bone, every single cell. My body responds to this loving attention by giving me vibrant health and aliveness.

I create peacefulness in my mind, and my body reflects this peacefulness as perfect health.

24   I TURN EVERY EXPERIENCE INTO AN OPPORTUNITY

When I experience a problem, and we all have them, I imme-diately say: OUT OF THIS SITUATION, ONLY GOOD WILL COME. THIS IS EASILY RESOLVED FOR THE HIGHEST GOOD OF ALL CONCERNED. ALL IS WELL AND I AM SAFE. I repeat this statement over and over. It keeps me calm and allows the Universe to find the best solu-tion. I am often amazed to see how quickly the issue can be resolved in a way that benefits everyone.

Each problem has a solution. All experiences are opportunities for me to learn and grow. I am safe.

25   I AM AT PEACE

Deep at the center of my being there is an infinite well of peace. Like a mountain lake deep and serene. No person, place, or outer chaos can touch me when I am in this space. In this space I am calm. I think clearly. I receive divine ideas. I am so peaceful.

Divine peace and harmony surround me and dwell in me. I feel tolerance, compassion, and love for all people, myself included.

26   I AM FLEXIBLE AND FLOWING

Life is a series of changes. Those of us who are rigid and inflexible in our thinking often snap when the winds of change blow. But those of us who are like willow trees bend eas-ily and adapt to the new changes. If we refuse to change, then Life passes us by, and we get left behind. Just as a flexible body is more comfortable to be in, so is a flexible mind more com-fortable to live in.

I am open to the new and changing. Every moment presents a wonderful new opportunity to become more of who I am. I flow with Life easily and effortlessly.

27 I NOW GO BEYOND OTHER PEOPLE'S FEARS AND LIMITATIONS

I am not my mother's fears and limitations, nor am I my father's fears and limitations. I am not even my own fears and limitations. These are only false thoughts that have been hanging around in my mind. I can erase them as easily as I can clean a dirty window. When the window of my mind is clean, I can clearly see the negative thoughts for what they are, and I can choose to eliminate them.

It is "my" mind that creates my experiences. I am unlimited in my own ability to create the good in my Life.

28 I AM WORTH LOVING

So many of us were taught conditional love. Therefore, we believe that we need to earn love. We feel that we are not lovable if we don't have a great job or a good relationship or a body like a model. This is nonsense. We do not have to earn the right to breathe. It is God given because we exist. So, too, is the right to love and be loved. The fact that we exist means that we are worth loving.

I do not have to earn love. I am lovable because I exist. Others reflect the love I have for myself.

29 MY THOUGHTS ARE CREATIVE

I have learned to love my thoughts; they are my best friends.

Say "Out!" to every negative thought that comes to my mind. No person, place, or thing has any power over me, for I am the only thinker in my mind. I create my own reality and everyone in it.

30   I AM AT PEACE WITH MY SEXUALITY

I believe that in many lifetimes I have experienced every sort of sexuality. I have been male and female, heterosexual and homosexual. Sometimes society has approved of my sexuality, and sometimes it has not. My sexuality has always been a learning experience for me, as it is in this lifetime. Yet, I know that my soul has no sexuality.

I rejoice in my sexuality and in my own body. My body is perfect for me in this lifetime. I embrace myself with love and compassion.

31   I AM AT PEACE WITH MY AGE

For me, it is always now. Yes, the numbers add up with time. But I feel as young or old as I choose to feel. There are people at 20 who are ancient, and there are people at 90 who are young. I know I came to this planet to experience every age, and they are all good. Each age unfolds into the next as easily as I allow it to happen. I keep my mind healthy and happy, and my body follows suit. I am at peace with where I am in time, and I look forward to all my precious days.

Each age has its own special joys and experiences. I am always the perfect age for where I am in Life.

32   THE PAST IS OVER

I cannot go back in time except in my mind. I can choose to replay yesterday if I want. But replaying yesterday takes away precious moments out of today—moments that once gone cannot be retrieved. So I let yesterday be gone, and I turn my total attention to this moment of today. This is my special moment, and I rejoice in it.

This is a new day. One that I have never lived before. I stay in the Now and enjoy each and every moment.

33   I RELEASE ALL CRITICISM

People who are self-righteous and judgmental have the most self-hatred of all. Because they refuse to change themselves, they point their fingers at everyone else. They see wrong everywhere. Because they are so critical, they attract much to criticize. One of the most important decisions we can make for our own spiritual growth is to totally release all criticism—of others, and most of all, of ourselves. We always have the option of thinking kind thoughts, unkind thoughts, or neutral thoughts. The more kind and loving thoughts we have, the more kindness and love we will attract in our lives.

I only give out that which I wish to receive in return. My love and acceptance of others is mirrored to me in every moment.

34   I AM WILLING TO LET GO

I know that each person has divine guidance and wisdom within them, so I do not have to run their lives for them. I am not here to control others. I am here to heal my own Life. People come into my Life at the right time, we share the time we are meant to have together, and then at the perfect time, they leave. I lovingly let go.

I release others to experience whatever is meaningful to them, and I am free to create that which is meaningful to me.

35 I SEE MY PARENTS AS TINY CHILDREN WHO NEED LOVE

When we have problems with our parents, we often forget that they too were once innocent babies. Who taught them to be hurtful? How can we help them heal their pain? We all need love and healing.

I have compassion for my parents' childhoods. I now know I chose them because they were perfect for what I had to learn. I forgive them and set them free, and I set myself free.

36 MY HOME IS A PEACEFUL HAVEN

Homes that are loved and appreciated radiate that love. Even if you are there for a short time, be sure you put your love into the rooms. And if you have a garage, put love there, too, and keep it neat and tidy. Hang a picture or something attractive, so when you first come home, you enter through beauty.

I bless my home with love. I put love in every corner, and my home lovingly responds with warmth and comfort. I am at peace.

37 AS I SAY "YES" TO LIFE, LIFE SAYS "YES" TO ME

Life has always said YES to you, even when you were creating negatively. Now that you are aware of this law of Life, you can choose to create your positive future.

Life mirrors my every thought. As I keep my thoughts positive, Life brings me only good experiences.

38   THERE IS PLENTY FOR EVERYONE, INCLUDING ME

There is so much food on this planet that we could feed every-one. Yes, there are people who are starving, but it is not the lack of food, it is the lack of love that allows this to happen. There is so much money and so many riches in the world—far more than we know. If it were all distributed equally, within a month or so, those who have money now would have more, and those who are now poor, would once again be poor. For wealth has to do with consciousness and deservability. There are billions of people on this planet, yet you will hear people tell you that they are lonely. If we don't reach out, love cannot find us. So, as I affirm my self-worth and my deservability, that which I need comes to me in the perfect time/space availability.

The Ocean of Life is lavish with its abundance. All my needs and desires are met before I even ask. My good comes from everywhere and everyone and everything.

39   ALL IS WELL IN MY WORLD

My Life has always worked perfectly, only I did not know it. I didn't realize that every negative event in my world was Life reflecting back to me my belief system. Now that I am aware, I can consciously program my thinking process to have a Life that works on all levels.

Everything in my Life works, now and forevermore.

40   MY WORK IS DEEPLY FULFILLING

When we learn to love what we do, then Life sees to it that we will always have interesting, creative occupations. When you are ready emotionally and mentally for the next step in Life, Life will move you to it. Give your best to Life today.

I do what I love and love what I do. I know that I am always working in the right place, with just the right people, and that I learn all of the valuable lessons my soul needs to learn.

41   LIFE SUPPORTS ME

When you follow the laws of Life, Life will support you abundantly.

Life created me to be fulfilled. I trust Life, and Life is always there at every turn. I am safe.

42   MY FUTURE IS GLORIOUS

Our futures will always represent our current thoughts. What you are thinking and saying right now is creating your future. So think glorious thoughts, and you will have a glorious future.

I now live in limitless love, light, and joy. All is well in my world.

43   I OPEN NEW DOORS TO LIFE

As I walk down the corridor of Life, there are doors on every side. Each one opens to a new experience. The more I clear the negative thought patterns from my mind, the more I find doors that open to only good experiences. My clarity of thinking brings to me the best that Life has to offer.

I rejoice in what I have, and I know fresh, new experiences are always ahead of me. I greet the new with open arms. I trust Life to be wonderful.

44 I CLAIM MY OWN POWER, AND I LOVINGLY CREATE MY OWN REALITY

No one can do it for you. Only you can make your own declarations in your mind. If you give your power to others, then you have none. When you claim your power, it is yours. Use it wisely.

I ask for more understanding so that I may knowingly and lovingly shape my world and my experiences.

45 I NOW CREATE A WONDERFUL NEW JOB

Bless your current job with love and release it with love to the next person who takes your place, knowing that you are moving into a new level of Life. Keep your affirmations for the new position clear and positive. And know that you deserve the best.

I am totally open and receptive to a wonderful new position, using my creative talents and abilities, working with and for people I love, in a wonderful location and earning good money.

46 EVERYTHING I TOUCH IS A SUCCESS

We always have the option of poverty thinking or prosperity thinking. When we think thoughts of lack and limitation, then that is what we experience. There is no way you can be prosperous if your thinking is impoverished. To be successful, you need to constantly think thoughts of prosperity and abundance.

I now establish a new awareness of success. I know I can be as successful as I make up my mind to be. I move into the Winning Circle. Golden opportunities are everywhere for me. Prosperity of every kind is drawn to me.

47 I AM OPEN AND RECEPTIVE TO NEW AVENUES OF INCOME

When we are open and receptive, Life will find many ways to bring income to us. As we know and affirm that we deserve all good, the one infinite source will open new channels. We often limit our own good by believing in fixed income and other closed ideas. Opening our consciousness opens the banks of heaven.

I now receive my good from expected and unexpected sources. I am an unlimited being, accepting from an unlimited source, in an unlimited way. I am blessed beyond my fondest dreams.

48 I DESERVE THE BEST AND I ACCEPT THE BEST NOW

The only thing that keeps us from having the good in our Life is that we don't believe we deserve it. Somewhere in childhood, we learned that we didn't deserve, and we believed it. Now it is the time to release that belief.

I am mentally and emotionally equipped to enjoy a prosperous and loving Life. It is my birthright to deserve all good. I claim my good.

49 LIFE IS SIMPLE AND EASY

The laws of Life are simple, far too simple for many people who want to struggle and complicate things. WHAT YOU GIVE

OUT COMES BACK TO YOU. WHAT YOU BELIEVE ABOUT YOURSELF AND ABOUT LIFE BECOMES TRUE FOR YOU. It is that simple.

All that I need to know at any give moment is revealed to me. I trust myself and I trust Life. All is well.

50 I AM TOTALLY ADEQUATE FOR ALL SITUATIONS

Know that you are far more than you think you are. You are divinely protected. You are connected with infinite wisdom. You are never alone. You have everything you need. Of course you are adequate for all situations.

I am one with the power and wisdom of the Universe. I claim this power, and it is easy for me to stand up for myself.

51 I LISTEN WITH LOVE TO MY BODY'S MESSAGES

At the first sign of the slightest dis-ease in your body, instead of giving money to the pharmaceutical companies, sit down, close your eyes, take three deep breaths, and go within, asking: WHAT IS IT I NEED TO KNOW? Because your body is trying to tell you something. If you rush to the medicine cabinet, you are, in effect, telling your body to SHUT UP! Please listen to your body; it loves you.

My body is always working toward optimum health. My body wants to be whole and healthy. I cooperate and become healthy, whole, and complete.

52 I EXPRESS MY CREATIVITY

Everyone has unique creativity within them. It is an act of loving ourselves to take the time to express this creativity no matter what it is. If we believe we are too busy to allow creative time, then we are missing a very fulfilling part of ourselves.

My unique creative talents and abilities flow through me and are expressed in deeply satisfying ways. My creativity is always in demand.

53 I AM IN THE PROCESS OF POSITIVE CHANGE

We are always in the process of change. I used to make many negative changes; now that I have learned to release old, outworn patterns, my changes are positive.

I am unfolding in fulfilling ways. Only good can come to me. I now express health, happiness, prosperity, and peace of mind.

54 I ACCEPT MY UNIQUENESS

No two snowflakes are alike, and no two daisies. Each person is a rare gem, with unique talents and abilities. We limit ourselves when we try to be like someone else. Rejoice in your uniqueness.

There is no competition and no comparison, for we are all different and meant to be that way. I am special and wonderful. I love myself.

55 ALL MY RELATIONSHIPS ARE HARMONIOUS

I see only harmony around me at all times. I willingly contribute to the harmony I desire. My Life is a joy.

When we create harmony in our minds and hearts,

we will find it in our lives. The inner creates the outer. Always.

56 *IT IS SAFE TO LOOK WITHIN*

We often are frightened to look within because we think that we will find this terrible being. But in spite of what "they" might have told us, what we will find is a beautiful child that longs for our love.

As I move through the layers of other people's opinions and beliefs, I see within myself a magnificent being—wise and beautiful. I love what I see in me.

57 *I EXPERIENCE LOVE WHEREVER I GO*

What we give out returns to us, multiplied and folded over. The best way to get love is to give love. Love can mean acceptance and support, comfort and compassion, kindness and gentleness. I certainly want to live in a world with these qualities.

Love is everywhere, and I am loving and lovable. Loving people fill my Life, and I find myself easily expressing love to others.

58 *LOVING OTHERS IS EASY WHEN I LOVE AND ACCEPT MYSELF*

We can't really love others until we love ourselves. Otherwise, what we call love is really co-dependency or addiction or neediness. No one can ever love you enough if you don't love yourself. You will always be saying things like: DO YOU REALLY LOVE ME? And there is no way you can satisfy another who does not love him- or herself. There will be pouty silences and jealousy. So learn to love yourself, and you will have a loving Life.

My heart is open. I allow my love to flow freely. I love myself. I love others, and others love me.

59   I AM BEAUTIFUL AND EVERYBODY LOVES ME

I use this affirmation a lot when I am walking down a city street. Even though they don't hear it, it is wonderful to see how many people respond to me with smiles. Try it. This affirmation can really make your day when you are out and about.

I radiate acceptance, and I am deeply loved by others. Love surrounds me and protects me.

60   I LOVE AND APPROVE OF MYSELF

Out of self-approval comes only good. We are not talking about vanity or pride, for those are just expressions of fear. Loving yourself means cherishing and appreciating the miracle that you are. You do have value and self-worth. Love being YOU!

I appreciate all that I do. I am good enough just as I am. I speak up for myself. I ask for what I want. I claim my power.

61   I AM A DECISIVE PERSON

It really is safe to make decisions. Make them with authority. If a decision turns out to be a poor one, then make another decision. Learn to turn within, and do a short meditation when you need a solution. You have all the answers within you. Practice going within often, and you will have a good, solid connection with your inner wisdom.

I trust my inner wisdom, and I make decisions with ease.

62   I AM ALWAYS SAFE WHEN I TRAVEL

You create your consciousness of safety, and of course, it will go with you everywhere—no matter what form of transportation you are using.

No matter what form of transportation I choose, I am safe and secure.

63   MY LEVEL OF UNDERSTANDING IS CONSTANTLY GROWING

When we understand more of Life, we experience more of Life's wonders. People who have a limited Life have a very limited understanding. They see things in black and white, yes or no, and they are usually motivated by fear or guilt. Allow your understanding to grow, and you will have a larger, more compassionate view of Life.

Each day I ask my Higher Self for the ability to deepen my understanding of Life and to move me beyond judgment and prejudice.

64   I NOW ACCEPT THE PERFECT MATE

Write down all the qualities you want in your ideal mate, and then check to make sure that you are expressing those qualities, too. You may need to make some inner changes before the right person can come in.

Divine Love now leads me to, and maintains me in, a loving relationship with my perfect mate.

65 SECURITY IS MINE NOW AND FOREVERMORE

Our belief systems are always evident in our experiences. As we create safety and security in our minds, then we find it in our world. Positive affirmations create a positive Life.

All that I have and all that I am is safe and secure. I live and move in a safe and secure world.

66 WORLD HEALING IS IN PROCESS NOW

Each one of us constantly contributes to world chaos or world peace. Every unkind, unloving, negative, fearful, judgmental, prejudicial thought contributes to the atmosphere that produces earthquakes, floods, drought, war, and other disasters. On the other hand, every loving, kind, peaceful, supportive, helpful thought contributes to the atmosphere that produces wellness and healing for all. What kind of world do you want to contribute to?

Every day I visualize our world as peaceful, whole, and healed. I see each person being well fed, clothed, and housed.

67 I BLESS OUR GOVERNMENT WITH LOVE

Our belief in a negative government produces just that. Do some positive affirmations for our government every day.

I affirm that each person in our government is loving, honest, honorable, and truly working for the betterment of all people.

68   *I LOVE MY FAMILY*

I have had hundreds of estranged families be lovingly reunited by doing this affirmation daily for three or four months. When we are estranged from our families, we often send a lot of negative energy back and forth. This affirmation stops that and opens the space for loving feelings to surface.

I have a loving, harmonious, joyous, healthy family; and we all have excellent communication.

69   *MY CHILDREN ARE DIVINELY PROTECTED*

If we are fearful for our children, they often give us things to worry about. We want our children to feel free and secure in the mental atmosphere we surround them with. So always do positive affirmations for your children when you are apart.

Divine wisdom resides within each of my children, and they are joyous, safe, and secure wherever they go.

70   *I LOVE ALL GOD'S CREATURES—ANIMALS GREAT AND SMALL*

Every creature, every insect, bird, and fish has its own special place in Life. They are just as important as we are.

I communicate easily and lovingly with all living beings, and know that they deserve our love and protection.

71   *I LOVE EXPERIENCING MY BABY'S BIRTH*

In the nine months before birth, talk and communicate with your baby. Prepare for the birthing experience so that it is a loving, easy experience for both of you. Describe the birth process to your baby in the most positive ways so that you can both cooperate with each other in supportive ways. Unborn children love to hear their mothers sing to them, and they love music, too.

The miracle of birth is a normal and natural process, and I go through it easily, effortlessly, and lovingly.

72   *I LOVE MY BABY*

I believe that we choose our parents, and we choose our children on a soul level. Our children have come to be our teachers. There is much we can learn from them. But most important is the love that can be shared.

My baby and I have a joyous, loving, peaceful relationship. We are a happy family.

73   *MY BODY IS FLEXIBLE*

Keeping my mind flexible and agile is reflected in the flexibility of my body. The only thing that keeps us rigid is fear. When we truly know that we are divinely protected and safe, then we can relax and just flow with the effortlessness of Life. Be sure to include dance time in your schedule.

Healing energy constantly flows through every organ and joint and cell. I move easily and effortlessly.

74   *I AM AWARE*

Several times a day, just stop and say to yourself: I AM AWARE! Then take a deep breath, and notice how much more you become aware of. There is always more to experience.

I constantly increase my awareness of myself, my body, and my Life. Awareness gives me the power to be in charge.

75   *I LOVE TO EXERCISE*

I expect to live a long time, and I want to run and dance and be flexible until my last day. My bones get stronger when I exercise, and I have found lots of different ways to enjoy movement of all kinds. Movement keeps us moving in Life.

Exercise helps to keep me young and healthy. My muscles love to move. I am an alive person.

76   *PROSPERITY IS MY DIVINE RIGHT*

Most people get quite angry when they hear that MONEY IS THE EASIEST THING TO DEMONSTRATE. But it is true. We must release our negative reactions to it and our negative beliefs about it first, though. I have found that it is easier to teach a workshop on sexuality than on money. People get incredibly angry when their beliefs about money are challenged. The people who want money the most fight the hardest to hold on to the limiting patterns. What is your negative belief about money that is keeping you from having some?

I deserve and willingly accept an abundance of prosperity flowing through my Life. I give and I receive joyously and lovingly.

77   *I AM CONNECTED WITH DIVINE WISDOM*

There is always an answer to every question. A solution to every problem. We are never lost, lonely, or abandoned in Life, for we have this infinite wisdom and guidance constantly with us. Learn to trust it, and you will feel safe all your Life.

Daily I go within to connect with all the wisdom of the Universe. I am constantly being led and guided in ways that are for my highest good and greatest joy.

78 TODAY I LOOK AT LIFE WITH FRESH EYES

When out-of-town people come to visit, they always help me to see my everyday world through their new eyes. We think we have seen it all, and yet we miss so much that is immediately around us. In my morning meditations, I ask to see more and to understand more this day. My world is infinitely larger than I know.

I am willing to see Life in a new and different way, to notice things that I have not noticed before. A new world awaits my new vision.

79 I AM IN STEP WITH TODAY

Within each and every one of us is the intelligence to understand and use all the new and exciting electronic wonders that are filling our lives. And if we do have difficulty programming our VCR or computer, all we have to do is ask a child. All the children of today are electronically literate. As it has been said before, "And the little children shall lead them."

I am open and receptive to the new in Life. I am willing to understand VCRs and computers and other wonderful electronic devices.

80 I MAINTAIN MY PERFECT WEIGHT

Junk foods and overly rich foods contribute to our ill health and overweight conditions. When we go for HEALTH and drop red meat and dairy and sugar and fat from our menus, then the body automatically goes to and settles at its perfect weight. Toxic bodies are fat. Healthy bodies are at the perfect weight. So, as we release toxic thoughts from our minds, our bodies respond by creating wellness and beauty.

My mind and my body are balanced and in tune. I achieve and maintain my perfect weight easily and effortlessly.

81 I AM IN TIP-TOP SHAPE

There was a time when we all ate natural, healthy foods. Today we have to pick our way between the junk and processed non-foods to find simple, healthy food. I have found that the simpler I eat, the healthier I am. Give your body the foods that grow, and you will grow.

I take loving care of my body. I eat healthful foods. I drink healthful beverages. My body responds by being in tip-top shape all the time.

82 MY ANIMALS ARE HEALTHY AND HAPPY

I refuse to feed my six wonderful animals any junk or canned foods. Their bodies are as important as mine. We all take good care of ourselves.

I lovingly communicate with my animals, and they let me know how I can make them happy, both mentally and physically. We live joyfully together. I am in harmony with all of Life.

83 I HAVE A NATURAL GREEN THUMB

I love the earth, and the earth loves me. I do everything I can to make it rich and productive.

Every plant I lovingly touch responds by growing forth in all its glory. House plants are happy. Flowers are vibrantly beautiful. Fruits and vegetables are abundant and delicious. I am in harmony with nature.

84 THIS IS A DAY OF GREAT HEALING

The mind that contributes to creating an illness is the same mind that can create wellness. The cells in our body are constantly responding to the mental atmosphere within us. Like people, they do their best work in a happy, loving environment. So fill your Life with joy, and you will be happy and healthy.

I connect with the healing energies of the Universe to heal myself and all those around me who are ready to be healed. I know that my mind is a powerful healing tool.

85 I LOVE AND RESPECT THE ELDERS IN MY LIFE

The way we treat elders now is the way we will be treated when we become older. I believe that our later years can become our treasure years, and we can all become ELDERS OF EXCELLENCE, living our lives in rich and full ways and contributing to the wellness of our society.

I treat the elders in my Life with the utmost love and respect, for I know that they are a wise and wonderful source of knowledge, experience, and truth.

86 MY VEHICLE IS A SAFE HAVEN FOR ME

I always send love to angry drivers on the road. I am aware that they don't know what they are doing to themselves. Anger creates angry situations. A long time ago, I gave up being angry at poor drivers. I am not going to ruin my day because you do not know how to drive. I bless my car with love and send love ahead of me on the road. Because I do this, I seldom have angry drivers around me. They are off causing trouble for other angry drivers. I lovingly share the road and almost always arrive right on time no matter what the traffic is. We take our consciousness everywhere; where you go, your mind goes. And it attracts like experiences.

When I am driving my vehicle, I am completely safe, relaxed, and comfortable. I bless the other drivers on the road with love.

87 MUSIC ENRICHES MY LIFE

We all dance to a different drummer and are fulfilled by different kinds of music. What is uplifting to one person can be a dreadful noise to another. I have a friend who plays meditation music for her trees, and it drives her neighbors nuts.

I fill my Life with harmonious and uplifting music that enriches my body and soul. Creative influences surround and inspire me.

88 I KNOW HOW TO QUIET MY THOUGHTS

Time alone and inner time gives us the chance to renew our spirits. And inner time gives us the guidance we need.

I deserve rest and quiet when I need it, and I create a space in my Life where I can go to get what I need. I am at peace with my solitude.

89 MY APPEARANCE REFLECTS MY LOVE OF SELF

Our clothes, our cars, and our homes reflect the way we feel about ourselves. A scattered mind will produce scattered objects everywhere. As we bring peace and harmony to our thoughts, our appearance and all our possessions automatically become harmonious and pleasing.

I groom myself well every morning and wear clothes that reflect my appreciation and love of Life. I am beautiful inside and out.

90   I HAVE ALL THE TIME IN THE WORLD

Time stretches when I need more and shrinks when I need less. Time is my servant, and I use it wisely. Here and now, in this moment, all is well.

I have plenty of time for each task that I need to perform today. I am a powerful person because I choose to live in the Present Moment.

91   I GIVE MYSELF A VACATION FROM WORK

We do our best work when we give ourselves short periods of rest. A five-minute break every two hours sharpens our minds. So too, vacation time benefits the mind and body. The workaholics who never rest or play become very intense people. They are seldom fun to be around. The child in us needs to play. If our inner child is not happy, then neither are we.

I plan vacations for myself in order to rest my mind and body. I stay within my budget and always have a wonderful time. I return to work relaxed and refreshed.

92   CHILDREN LOVE ME

We need contact with all the generations. Senior condos and retirement communities lack the laughter of children. Connecting with children keeps us young at heart. The little child in us loves to play with children.

Children love me, and they fcel safe around me. I let them come and go freely. My adult self feels appreciated and inspired by children.

93   MY DREAMS ARE A SOURCE OF WISDOM

I always go to sleep with loving thoughts to lay the groundwork for the work I do in my dreams. Loving thoughts bring loving answers.

I know that many of the questions I have about Life can be answered as I sleep. I clearly remember my dreams when I wake up each morning.

94   I SURROUND MYSELF WITH POSITIVE PEOPLE

When we allow negative people to fill our lives, it becomes much harder to stay positive ourselves. So don't allow yourself to be dragged down with other people's negative thinking. Choose your friends with care.

My friends and relatives exude love and positive energy, and I return these feelings. I know that I may have to release people from my Life who are not supportive of me.

95   I MANAGE MY FINANCES WITH LOVE

Every bill you pay is evidence that someone trusted in your ability to earn the money. So sprinkle love in all your financial transactions, including the IRS. Think of taxes as paying rent to the country.

I write my checks and pay my bills with gratitude and love. I always have enough money in my bank account to take care of the necessities and luxuries in my Life.

96 I LOVE MY INNER CHILD

Daily connection with our inner child, the little one you once were, contributes to our wellness. At least once a week, take your inner child by the hand and spend some time with it. Do some special things together—things you loved to do when you were little.

The child in me knows how to play and love and wonder. As I support this part of me, it opens the door to my heart, and my Life is enriched.

97 I ASK FOR HELP WHEN I NEED IT

Ask and ye shall receive. The Universe lies in smiling repose, waiting for me to ask.

It is easy for me to ask for help when I need it. I feel safe in the midst of change, knowing that change is a natural law of Life. I am open to the love and support of others.

98 HOLIDAYS ARE A TIME OF LOVE AND JOY

Gifts are wonderful to exchange, but even greater is the love you can share with everyone you meet.

Celebrating holidays with my family and friends is always enjoyable. We always make time for laughter, and express gratitude for the many blessings of Life.

99 I AM PATIENT AND KIND WITH ALL WHOM I ENCOUNTER EACH DAY

Try thanking everyone you meet today for something. You will be delighted with how much it means to them. You will receive more than you give.

I beam kind and loving thoughts to store clerks, restaurant workers, law enforcement personnel, and all others whom I encounter during the day. All is well in my world.

100 I AM AN EMPATHETIC FRIEND

When a friend comes to you with a problem, it doesn't necessarily mean they want you to fix it. Probably all they want is a sympathetic ear. A good listener is a valuable friend.

I am in tune with other people's thoughts and emotions. I give advice and support to my friends when they ask for it, and just listen with love when that is appropriate.

101 MY PLANET IS IMPORTANT TO ME

Loving the earth is something we can all do. Our beautiful earth provides everything we need, and we need to honor her at all times. Saying a small prayer for the earth every day is a loving thing to do. The health of this planet is very important. If we do not take care of our planet, where will we live?

I bless this planet with love. I nourish the vegetation. I am kind to the creatures. I keep the air clean. I eat natural food and use natural products. I am deeply grateful for, and appreciative of, being alive. I contribute to harmony, wholeness, and healing. I know peace begins with me. I love my Life. I love my world.

Thank you for letting me share some ideas with you!

And so it is!

❦   ❦   ❦

RECOMMENDED READING

Ageless Body, Timeless Mind—Deepak Chopra, M.D.

Aging Parents & You—Eugenia Anderson-Ellis

Alternative Medicine, the Definitive Guide—The Burton Goldberg Group

As Someone Dies—Elizabeth A. Johnson

Autobiography of a Yogi—Paramahansa Yogananda

Between Parent and Child—Hiam Ginott

The Canary and Chronic Fatigue—Majid Ali, M.D.

The Celestine Prophecy—James Redfield

The Complete Book of Essential Oils & Aromatherapy—Valerie Ann Worwood

Constant Craving: What Your Food Cravings Mean and How to Overcome Them—Doreen Virtue, Ph.D.

Cooking for Healthy Healing—Linda G. Rector-Page, N.D., Ph.D.

The Course in Miracles—Foundation for Inner Peace

Creative Visualization—Shakti Gawain

Diet for a New America—John Robbins

Discovering the Child Within—John Bradshaw

Do What You Love, the Money Will Follow—Marsha Sinetar

The Earth Adventure: Your Soul's Journey Through Personal Reality—Ron Scolastico, Ph.D.

Everyday Wisdom—Dr. Wayne W. Dyer

Feel the Fear and Do It Anyway—Susan Jeffers, Ph.D.

Fire in the Soul—Joan Borysenko, Ph.D.

Fit for Life—Harvey and Marilyn Diamond

The Fountain of Age—Betty Friedan

Great American Cookbook—Marilyn Diamond

Handbook to Higher Consciousness—Ken Keyes

Healing the Heart, Healing the Body—Ron Scolastico, Ph.D.

Healthy Healing, An Alternative Healing Reference—Linda G. Rector-Page, N.D., Ph.D.

The Heroic Path: One Woman's Journey from Cancer to Self-Healing—Angela Passidomo Trafford

How to Meditate—Lawrence LeShan

Instead of Therapy: Help Yourself Change and Change the Help You're Getting—Tom Rusk, M.D.

Learning to Love Yourself—Sharon Wegscheider-Cruse

Life After Life—Raymond Moody, M.D.

Lifegoals—Amy E. Dean

Life! You Wanna Make Something of It?—Tom Costa, M.D.

Losing Your Pounds of Pain: Breaking the Link Between Abuse, Stress, and Overeating—Doreen Virtue, Ph.D.

Love Is Letting Go of Fear—Gerald Jampolsky, M.D.

Love, Medicine, and Miracles—Bernie Siegel, M.D.

Man's Search for Meaning—Viktor Frankl

Many Lives, Many Masters—Brian Weiss, M.D.

The Menopause Industry: How the Medical Establishment Exploits Women—Sandra Coney

Minding the Body, Mending the Mind—Joan Borysenko, Ph.D.

Mutant Message, Down Under—Marlo Morgan

My Mother Made Me Do It—Nan Kathryn Fuchs

The Nature of Personal Reality—Jane Roberts

Opening Our Hearts to Men—Susan Jeffers, Ph.D.

Parents' Nutrition Bible—Dr. Earl Mindell, R.Ph., Ph.D.

Passages—Gail Sheehy

Peace, Love, and Healing—Bernie Siegel, M.D.

The Power of 5—Harold Bloomfield, M.D., and Robert K. Cooper, Ph.D.

The Power of the Mind to Heal—Joan and Miroslav Borysenko, Ph.D.'s

The Power of Touch—Phyllis K. Davis

Prescription for Nutritional Healing—James F. Balch, M.D., and Phyllis A. Balch, C.N.C.

Real Magic—Dr. Wayne W. Dyer

The Relaxation Response—Benson and Klipper

A Return to Love—Marianne Williamson

Revolution from Within—Gloria Steinem

The Road Less Traveled—M. Scott Peck, M.D.

Saved by the Light—Dannion Brinkley

The Science of Mind—Ernest Holmes

Self-Parenting—John Pollard III

Staying on the Path—Dr. Wayne W. Dyer

Super Nutrition Gardening—Dr. William S. Peavy and Warren Peary

Thoughts of Power and Love—Susan Jeffers, Ph.D.

The Tibetan Book of Living and Dying—Sogyal Rinpoche

What Do You Really Want for Your Children?—Dr. Wayne W. Dyer

What Every Woman Needs to Know Before (and After) She Gets Involved with Men and Money—Judge Lois Forer

When 9 to 5 Isn't Enough—Marcia Perkins-Reed

Woman Heal Thyself: An Ancient Healing System for Contemporary Woman—Jeanne Elizabeth Blum

A Woman's Worth—Marianne Williamson

Women Alone: Creating a Joyous and Fulfilling Life—Julie Keene and Ione Jenson

Women Who Love Too Much—Robin Norwood

Your Companion to 12 Step Recovery—Robert Odom

Your Sacred Self—Dr. Wayne W. Dyer

❦ Any book by Emmett Fox or Dr. John MacDonald

❦ Also, the audiocassette program, *Making Relationships Work*, by Barbara De Angelis, Ph.D.

SELF-HELP RESOURCES

The following list of resources can be used for more information about recovery options for addictions, health problems, or problems related to dysfunctional families. The addresses and telephone numbers listed are for the national headquarters; look in your local yellow pages under "Community Services" for resources closer to your area.

In addition to the following groups, other self-help organizations may be available in your area to assist your healing and recovery for a particular Life crisis not listed here. Consult your telephone directory, call a counseling center or help line near you, or write or call:

American Self-Help Clearinghouse
St. Clares-Riverside Medical Center
Denville, NJ 07834
(201) 625-7101
(8:30am - 5:00pm Eastern Time)

National Self-Help Clearinghouse
25 West 43rd Street, Room 620
New York, NY 10036
(212) 642-2944

AIDS

AIDS Hotline
(800) 342-2437

Children with AIDS
Project of America
4020 N. 20th Street, Ste. 101
Phoenix, AZ 85016
(602) 265-4859
Hotline
(602) 843-8654

National AIDS Network
(800) 342-2437

Project Inform
19655 Market Street, Ste. 220
San Francisco, CA 94103
(415) 558-8669

Spanish AIDS Hotline
(800) 344-7432

TDD (Hearing Impaired) AIDS
Hotline: (800) 243-7889

The Names Project – AIDS Quilt
(800) 872-6263

ALCOHOL ABUSE

Al-Anon Family Headquarters
200 Park Avenue South
New York, NY 10003
(212) 302-7240

Alcoholics Anonymous (AA)
General Service Office
475 Riverside Drive
New York, NY 10115
(212) 870-3400

Children of Alcoholics Foundation
P.O. Box 4185
Grand Central Station
New York, NY 10163-4185
(212) 754-0656
(800) 359-COAF

Meridian Council, Inc.
Administrative Offices
4 Elmcrest Terrace
Norwalk, CT 06850

National Association of Children of Alcoholics (NACOA)
11426 Rockville Pike, Ste. 100
Rockville, MD 20852
(301) 468-0985

National Clearinghouse for Alcohol and Drug Information (NCADI)
P.O. Box 234
Rockville, MD 20852
(301) 468-2600

National Council on Alcoholism and Drug Dependency (NCADD)
12 West 21st Street
New York, NY 10010
(212) 206-6770

ANOREXIA/BULIMIA

American Anorexia/Bulimia Association, Inc.
418 East 76th Street
New York, NY 10021
(212) 891-8686

Bulimic/Anorexic Self-Help (BASH)
P.O. Box 39903
St. Louis, MO 63138
(800) 888-4680

Eating Disorder Organization
1925 East Dublin Granville Road
Columbus, OH 43229-3517
(614) 436-1112

CANCER

National Cancer Institute
(800) 4-CANCER

Commonweal
P.O. Box 316
Bolinas, CA 94924
(415) 868-0971

ECAP (Exceptional Cancer Patients)
Bernie S. Siegel, M.D.
300 Plaza Middlesex
Middletown, CT 06457
(800) 700-8869

CHILD MOLESTATION

Adults Molested As Children United (AMACU)
232 East Gish Road
San Jose, CA 95112
(800) 422-4453

Childhelp National Headquaters
6463 Independence Avenue
Woodland Hills, CA 91367
(818) 347-7280

National Committee for Prevention of Child Abuse
322 South Michigan Avenue, Ste. 1600
Chicago, IL 60604
(312) 663-3520

CHILDREN'S AND TEENS' CRISIS INTERVENTION

Boy's Town Crisis Hotline
(800) 448-3000

Covenant House Hotline
(800) 999-9999

Kid Save
(800) 543-7283

National Runaway and Suicide Hotline
(800) 621-4000

CO-DEPENDENCY

Co-Dependents Anonymous
P.O. Box 33577
Phoenix, AZ 85067-3577
(602) 277-7991

DEBTS

Debtors Anonymous
General Service Office
P.O. Box 400
Grand Central Station
New York, NY 10163-0400
(212) 642-8220

DIABETES

American Diabetes Association
(800) 232-3472

DRUG ABUSE

Cocaine Anonymous
(800) 347-8998

National Cocaine-Abuse Hotline
(800) 262-2463
(800) COCAINE

National Institute of Drug Abuse (NIDA)
Parklawn Building
5600 Fishers Lane, Room 10A-39
Rockville, MD 20852
(301) 443-6245 (for information)
(800) 662-4357 (for help)

World Service Office (NA)
P.O. Box 9999
Van Nuys, CA 91409
(818) 780-3951

EATING DISORDERS

Food Addiction Hotline
Florida Institute of Technology
FIT Hotline
Drug Addiction & Depression
(800) 872-0088

Overeaters Anonymous
National Office
Rio Rancho, NM
(505) 891-2664

GAMBLING

Gamblers Anonymous
National Council on Compulsive
Gambling
444 West 59th Street, Room 1521
New York, NY 10019
(212) 265-8600

GRIEF

Grief Recovery Helpline
(800) 445-4808

Grief Recovery Institute
8306 Wilshire Blvd., Ste. 21A
Beverly Hills, CA 90211
(213) 650-1234

HEALTH ISSUES

Alzheimer's Disease Information
(800) 621-0379

American Chronic Pain Association
P.O. Box 850
Rocklin, CA 95677
(916) 632-0922

American Foundation of Traditional Chinese Medicine
1280 Columbus Avenue, Ste. 302
San Francisco, CA 94133
(415) 776-0502

American Holistic Health Association
P.O. Box 17400
Anaheim, CA 92817
(714) 779-6152

The Fetzer Institute
9292 West KL Avenue
Kalamazoo, MI 49009
(616) 375-2000

Hippocrates Health Institute
1443 Palmdale Court
West Palm Beach, Fl 33411
(407) 471-8876

Hospicelink
(800) 331-1620

Institute for Human Potential and Mind-Body Medicine
Deepak Chopra, M.D.
1110 Camino Del Mar, Ste. G
Del Mar, CA 92014
(619) 794-2425

Institute for Noetic Sciences
P.O. Box 909, Dept. M
Sausalito, CA 94966-0909
(800) 383-1394

The Mind-Body Medical Institute
185 Pilgrim Road
Boston, MA 02215
(617) 732-7000

National Health Information Center
P.O. Box 1133
Washington, DC 20013-1133
(800) 336-4797

Optimum Health Care Institute
6970 Central Avenue
Lemon Grove, CA 91945
(619) 464-3346

Preventive Medicine Institute
Dean Ornish, M.D.
900 Bridgeway, Ste. 2
Sausalito, CA 94965
(415) 332–2525

World Research Foundation
15300 Ventura Blvd., Ste. 405
Sherman Oaks, CA 91403
(818) 907-5483

IMPOTENCE

Impotency Institute of America
2020 Pennsylvania Avenue N.W.,
Ste. 292
Washington, DC 20006
(800) 669-1603

INCEST

Incest Survivors Resource Network International, Inc.
P.O. Box 7375
Las Cruces, NM 88006-7375
(505) 521-4260

MISSING CHILDREN

National Center for Missing and Exploited Children
(800) 843-5678

RAPE

Austin Rape Crisis Center
1824 East Oltorf
Austin, TX 78741
(512) 440-7273

SEX ADDICTIONS

National Council on Sexual Addictions
P.O. Box 652
Azle, TX 76098-0652
(800) 321-2066

SMOKING ABUSE

Nicotine Anonymous
2118 Greenwich Street
San Francisco, CA 94123
(415) 750-0328

SPOUSAL ABUSE

National Coalition Against Domestic Violence
P.O. Box 34103
Washington, DC 20043-4103
(202) 638-6388
(800) 333-7233 (crisis line)

STRESS REDUCTION

The Biofeedback & Psychophysiology Clinic
The Menninger Clinic
P.O. Box 829
Topeka, KS 66601-0829
(913) 273-7500

Rise Institute
P.O. Box 2733
Petaluma, CA 94973
(707) 765-2758

The Stress Reduction Clinic
Jon Kabat-Zinn, Ph.D.
University of Massachusetts
Medical Center
55 Lake Avenue North
Worcester, MA 01655
(508) 856-1616

ABOUT THE AUTHOR

Louise L. Hay is a metaphysical teacher and lecturer and the bestselling author of 15 books, including *You Can Heal Your Life, Meditations to Heal Your Life,* and *The Power Is Within You.* Since beginning her career as a Science of Mind minister in 1981, she has assisted thousands of people in discovering and using the full potential of their own creative powers for personal growth and self-healing. Louise's works have been translated into 23 different languages in 30 countries throughout the world. She makes her home near San Diego, California.

We hope you enjoyed this Hay House book.

If you would like to receive a free catalog
featuring additional Hay House books
and products, or if you would like information
about the Hay Foundation, please write to:

Hay House, Inc.
1154 E. Dominguez St.
P.O. Box 6204
Carson, CA 90749-6204
or call:
(800) 654-5126